Good
Old-Fashioned
Cakes

D1254740

To Mike —
From Debbie
Christmas 1990

Good Old-Fashioned Cakes

More than Seventy Classic Cake Recipes–Updated for Today's Bakers

Susan Kosoff

Illustrations by Diana Thewlis

St. Martin's Press   New York

GOOD OLD-FASHIONED CAKES. Text copyright © 1989 by Susan Kosoff. Illustrations copyright © 1989 by Diana Thewlis. All rights reserved. Printed in the United States of America. No part of this book may be used or reproduced in any manner whatsoever without written permission except in the case of brief quotations embodied in critical articles or reviews. For information, address St. Martin's Press, 175 Fifth Avenue, New York, N.Y. 10010.

Design by Judith A. Stagnitto

Library of Congress Cataloging-in-Publication Data

Kosoff, Susan.
    Good old-fashioned cakes/Susan Kosoff.
       p.   cm.
    ISBN 0-312-02922-5
    1. Cake. I. Title.
TX771.K64   1989
641.8′653—dc19   89-30138
                               CIP

10 9 8 7 6 5 4 3 2

Dedicated to my son, Mark Landsman, with love from the tippy, tippy top of the sky, and to my husband, Paul, from the bottom of my heart.

Very special thanks to Beth Backman, Lorna Vanterpool, Amy Kaplan, Valerie Brissett, Robert Fischel, Deborah Mintcheff, Danny Abelson, and Suzanne Zavrian.

HER FIRST ATTEMPT

She measured out the butter
   with a very solemn air;
The milk and sugar also, and
   she took the greatest care
To count the eggs correctly and
   to add a little bit
Of baking powder, which you
   know, beginners oft omit
Then she stirred it all together
   and she baked it full an hour
But she never quite forgave
   herself for leaving out the
          flour.

Excerpt from a World War I–era
Davis Baking Powder Booklet

Contents

Introduction

Just about all the bakers I know bake because their mother, grandmother, or Great-aunt Betty taught them the basics at a very early age. I made my first "cake" when I was ten. It was my mother's recipe and my favorite dessert: homemade chocolate pudding spread between layers of cinnamon-flavored graham crackers, chilled until icy cold, and topped with freshly whipped cream. This old-fashioned refrigerator or icebox cake is not exactly a traditional cake, but Mom, an inventive and creative cook, has never been a traditional baker. In fact, I'm not revealing any family secrets when I say that Mom has never baked. Before I embarked on a culinary career, most of what I learned about baking I taught myself or picked up by peering over the shoulders of sympathetic aunts and friendly neighbors.

The tradition of sharing recipes, as well as the experience and expertise of the baker, dates back to the time when original recipes were handwritten and passed down from generation to generation. Hands-on experience was invaluable to the new baker, since cookbook recipes were often vague and incomplete. It was common for a recipe to read like the one I found in a handwritten cookbook in the vaults of the Stockbridge, Massachusetts, library: "Take 2 tea cups of sugar, butter the size of 2 eggs, 2 or 3 eggs, 1 coffee cup sour milk with 2 teaspoons soda added, salt, flavoring and flour enough to make a good batter to bake. Bake until done."

Baking, it turns out, was a real challenge to our foremothers. Ingredients weren't neatly packaged as we know them today, ready to pour or sprinkle. Great-Grandmama's sugar was delivered to her in large cones or loaves, sometimes two or three feet high and weighing anywhere from 12 to 50 pounds. Before using it, she had to knock a chunk from the cone with a hammer and then pound it into granules! Ovens weren't regulated until the twentieth century, and because there was no electricity, everything had to be done by hand. Still, she overcame the obstacles and pounded, whipped, and beat those cakes (often all day long) until they became light and fluffy—and, ultimately, unforgettable to anyone who tasted them.

The selection of recipes in this book pays tribute to those old-fashioned, original home-baked classics, including devil's food cake (page 59), applesauce cake (page 41), Old-fashioned Yankee Pound Cake (page 50), Lemon Pudding Cake (page 120), and strawberry shortcake (page 100). All of the following recipes have been tested, rewritten, and prepared with easy-to-find ingredients, using an electric mixer. (Grandma's muscles aren't necessary to master cake-making anymore!) You'll also find information on ingredients, equipment, and baking techniques, as well as hints, tips, and secrets that will ensure every cake you bake is a stunning success. So even without years of experience, or an experienced baker in the house, you can still turn out a great-tasting, great-looking cake you'll be proud to serve. Even to Grandma.

Before You Begin

Read carefully through this entire chapter. It explains everything you need to know about making the cakes in this book. You don't have to be an experienced baker, cook, or food chemist to make a good-tasting cake. In fact, baking a cake is a "piece of cake" when you have a recipe you can rely on, impeccably fresh ingredients, the proper pan, an accurate oven, and a few techniques tucked under your apron. The following list will get you organized before you begin baking, but the most important thing for you to do before starting a recipe is to **read it through before you begin.** This means the entire recipe, not just part of it!

1. Assemble the ingredients.   The recipe will list all the ingredients you need. Make sure you have everything you need *before* you start to bake, then measure and organize the ingredients so that they are in the order called for in the recipe. If the recipe requires chopped nuts, melted chocolate, beaten eggs, or other easily prepared ingredients, carry out these small tasks before you start to incorporate other ingredients.

A cake will have better volume if you allow eggs, milk, butter, and other refrigerated ingredients listed in the recipe to warm to room temperature (about 70°F) before using. If you have the 30 minutes it requires—great. If not, here are a few tricks to speed up the process:

- Soften cold or frozen butter quickly by grating on a coarse grater or, with a sharp knife, cutting the butter into small pieces. Let it stand at room temperature for 5 to 10 minutes before using.
- Bring unshelled eggs to room temperature by soaking in hot tap water 3 to 5 minutes.
- Warm dairy products in a saucepan over very low heat for 1 minute, or until tepid; or place in a microwave-safe container and heat about 20 seconds at high power.

2. Preheat the oven.   At least 15 minutes before you plan to bake the cake, position the oven rack(s) as directed in the recipe. Place an oven thermometer in the center of the rack; set the dial to the required temperature, adjusting it if necessary to achieve the desired temperature, and wait until the temperature is correct before putting the cake in the oven.

3. Prepare the pan. Each recipe specifies the number, type, and pan size you'll need, as well as directions on how to prepare the pan before filling it with batter. This is what you should do if the recipe states the following:

"Grease; dust with flour." Using an empty butter wrapper or a piece of paper towel, generously spread softened butter or solid shortening all over the bottom and sides of the pan; dust the entire surface lightly with flour, shaking out any excess. Avoid coating with too much flour—it creates a thick, unattractive crust during baking.

"Grease; line with waxed paper; grease waxed paper; dust with flour." Grease the pan as described above; cut a piece of waxed paper to fit the bottom of the pan and press it smoothly into the greased pan. Spread additional butter over waxed paper and dust with flour as described above.

"Ungreased." Angel food, chiffon, and some sponge cakes need to cling to the sides of the pan in order to rise to their full height in the oven; grease and flour get in their way. Do nothing to the pan, but make sure it's spotlessly clean and dry.

4. Follow the recipe steps in the order stated. The texture of a cake depends, in part, on the techniques and methods you use to mix together the ingredients. Always follow the directions in the order in which they are written.

Ingredients and What They Do

Cake ingredients are somewhat like actors in a play—each performs a specific role, and all are important to the final production. Use only the freshest, highest-quality ingredients available, and always sniff or taste them just before using— one funny flavor, and your cake won't be worth eating.

Main Ingredients

Air and steam. The first ingredients on the list, and you can't even measure or taste them! Air is that elusive commodity largely responsible for leavening cakes, giving them volume and texture. When you cream butter, beat egg whites, or simply stir the batter (see "Techniques," pages 13–16 for details), air bubbles are formed and trapped in the batter. Later, while the cake bakes, the heat in the oven converts the liquid in the batter to steam through those air bubbles, helping to expand and leaven the cake. Some cakes, such as angel food and true sponge cakes, rely solely on air and steam for leavening power (others, such as butter or chiffon cakes, rely on chemical leaveners as well). What's most important to remember about air is that it's fragile and temperamental. It collapses if it's not pampered or handled gently after being incorporated into the batter, and it won't stand around for a long time, waiting for you to get it into the oven!

Baking powder. An invention of the nineteenth century, baking powder is a chemical leavener that produces carbon dioxide gas. It's composed of an alkali substance (bicarbonate of soda) and an acid in the form of salt crystals (calcium acid phosphate). Originally, baking powder was "single acting," which means the chemical reaction (release of carbon dioxide gas) occurs as soon as the baking powder is mixed with the liquid in the batter. Today, the most common baking powder available is composed of sodium aluminum sulfate-phosphate combinations. The chemical reaction of this "double-acting" baking powder is slower, allowing the reaction to occur twice—first when combined with liquid ingredients in the batter, and again when placed in the hot oven. Too much baking powder causes a cake to expand and collapse, while too little or old baking powder produces a cake with an overly compact crumb and poor volume.

Always use *double-acting* baking powder for these recipes. If you're bothered by

3

the slight aluminum aftertaste (most people can't taste it), bake with aluminum-free baking powder. You'll find it in some supermarkets and most health-food stores. Whatever type you choose, buy small quantities and use within six months.

Baking soda. When an acid ingredient such as buttermilk, sour cream, yogurt, or molasses is included in a cake, another leavening agent, baking soda (an alkali), is added to balance the acid-alkali reaction and to achieve optimal leavening power. Mixed together, the acid and alkali ingredients react chemically to produce carbon dioxide gas and cause leavening. Baking soda works quickly and only once; because it lacks the double action of baking powder, work quickly if your cake contains baking soda and don't delay putting it into the oven. Before you measure baking soda, eliminate any lumps by stirring it first, or shaking it through a small, fine-meshed strainer.

Eggs. Eggs add liquid, flavor, color, and texture to cakes, and act as aerating leaveners as well. When beaten, either whole or separately, eggs trap air bubbles. Later, in the hot oven, these bubbles convert the moisture of the eggs into steam, and the batter expands. Simultaneously, the heat coagulates the protein of the eggs, which strengthens the structure of the cake. For these recipes use fresh, *large* USDA eggs only; the color of the eggshell does not matter.

Fat. Fat contributes texture, flavor, and freshness. When a recipe calls for *butter,* use the *freshest, sweetest butter* available. I use Land O'Lakes for its superb flavor and solid fat content. When creamed, butter has the capacity to trap air. As other ingredients are incorporated into the batter, the fat particles stay suspended and help distribute the ingredients evenly throughout. During baking, the melting fat permits the trapped gases to explode, weakening the starch proteins and producing a tender cake. *Salted butter* may be substituted as a last resort; but since salt acts as a preservative, it's often difficult to determine whether the butter really is fresh. If salted butter is the only butter available to you, just omit the salt from the recipe and hope for the best. *Solid shortening* was often used in old-fashioned cakes and produces a very tender cake, but the flavor falls short of butter. *Margarine,* which contains less fat, and even less flavor than butter, is not recommended for these recipes (except for recipes in "Modern Day Classic Cakes" that specifically call for soy margarine, which can be purchased in most health-food stores). *Packaged whipped butter* is not considered a substitute for blocks or sticks of butter. *Oil* is used in chiffon cakes and in some other recipes, but it should not be substituted for butter.

Flour. Flour forms the framework of a cake. It's milled from wheat kernels, which are composed of three principal parts: the bran, the germ, and the endosperm. Wheat is categorized as either hard or soft, depending on when it is harvested, but the major difference between the types is their protein and starch levels. Both contain protein and starch, but hard wheat contains a higher percentage of protein. When mixed with liquid, the protein swells and forms gluten. During baking, and with the help of leaveners in the cake, gluten casts the crumb structure of the cake. Soft wheat contains less protein and more starch; it absorbs fat and moisture more quickly, producing a softer, more velvety crumb.

Each recipe specifies the type of flour to use. *Bread, self-rising,* or *instant-blending flour* is not considered a substitute for any of the flours used in these recipes.

All-purpose flour is produced by removing the bran and the germ and milling only the endosperm. It's milled from a blend of high-protein hard wheat and lower-protein soft wheat. The combination of soft and hard wheats produces a flour of medium wheat suitable for general usage. Since the protein content of all-purpose flour may vary from miller to miller, check the nutrition labeling before purchasing, and choose flour with 11 to 14 grams of protein per cup.

Bleached all-purpose flour has been treated chemically to remove any pigmentation.

Unbleached all-purpose flour is a blend of hard and soft wheats that has not been treated chemically.

Cake flour is milled from soft-wheat flour only and produces a cake with a more delicate and finer-textured crumb. It packs easily, and I suggest sifting it before measuring for accurate results. Do not substitute *self-rising* cake flour for these recipes.

Whole wheat flour is milled from a hard wheat and is just what it's name implies. It includes the entire kernel, not just the endosperm. Because the germ contains fat, whole wheat flour should be stored in the refrigerator to prolong freshness.

Whole wheat pastry flour is milled from a soft-wheat flour and produces a finer-textured crumb. Store in the refrigerator for maximum freshness.

Milk and other liquids.   Milk, buttermilk, sour cream, yogurt, and water are the most common liquids used in cakes. Liquids help to dissolve sugar, develop gluten in flour, and form steam in the oven. Milk and other dairy products add flavor and color as well. When the recipes in this book call for milk, use whole milk.

Sugar and other sweeteners.   Sugar contributes flavor to a cake and helps brown the crust during baking. Sugar also acts as a tenderizer because it helps incorporate air into fat, as well as having a softening effect on gluten, the protein formed when flour and liquid are mixed. Use *granulated sugar* in the recipes in this book, unless otherwise stated.

Brown sugar is processed sugar with molasses added to it. It's available in two forms—light and dark (the dark has a more distinctive flavor). The recipe will state my preference, but you may always substitute equal amounts of one for the other.

Confectioners' sugar is pulverized granulated sugar with added cornstarch, and is commonly known as *powdered sugar*. It's mainly used to dust cakes and make icings. Although the recipe for Angel Food Cake (page 72) includes it as a main ingredient, confectioners' sugar should not be substituted in other recipes for granulated or brown sugar.

Honey, maple syrup, unsulphured molasses, and light or dark corn syrup are used for their distinctive flavor. Do not substitute other sugars for them.

Other Ingredients

Chocolate.   This is used for baking and decoration. Both *unsweetened* and *semisweet* chocolate are conveniently packaged in boxes containing eight 1-ounce squares. I use Nestlé, Baker's, or Hershey's. Use whatever brand you prefer, but make sure that it's *real* chocolate and not a chocolate-flavored substitute.

Chocolate chips are used for glazes and decorations or are stirred whole into batter.

For optimal freshness, store all chocolate wrapped in an airtight container at room temperature.

Coconut.   Although freshly grated coconut is decidedly more delicious and less sweet, flaked coconut packaged in airtight bags or vacuum-sealed cans is acceptable.

Cream of tartar.   Cream of tartar stabilizes beaten egg whites and helps prevent them from deflating. If you don't have it on your pantry shelf, substitute 1 teaspoon fresh lemon juice or a pinch of salt for every 3 egg whites used in the recipe. When making Angel Food Cake (page 72), make no substitutions; cream of tartar is used to whiten the crumb as well.

Dried fruits.   This includes *apples, apricots, figs, dates, currants,* and dark and golden *raisins*. Always use dried fruits that are soft—hard fruit will not soften during baking.

To soften hard raisins, place them in a bowl with enough boiling water to cover. Soak raisins about 10 minutes or until softened; pat dry before using.

To restore other hard, dried fruit, soak briefly in boiling water just until tender; drain, pat dry, and allow to air-dry completely.

Extracts and other flavorings.   Read the labels carefully when buying vanilla and almond extracts and select only *pure* extracts, not imitations. The cost is noticeably different, but so is the flavor.

Fruit peel means freshly grated lemon or orange peel. The dehydrated bottled version is unacceptable.

Salt is the one ingredient that has the unique ability to emphasize other flavors in a cake.

Nuts.   This family includes *almonds, walnuts, pistachios, hazelnuts, macadamias,* and *pecans.* To keep nuts fresh, store them in an airtight container in the refrigerator or freezer. Bring to room temperature, and always taste them just before using to make sure they're fresh.

Spices.   When a recipe in this book calls for a spice, it means *ground,* not whole, spice. This includes *cinnamon, ginger, nutmeg* (preferably freshly grated), *allspice, cloves, cardamom,* and *mace.* Ground spices lose their fragrance within six to nine months, or sooner than that if stored near heat.

Unsweetened cocoa powder.   Use *real* cocoa powder (such as Hershey's or Droste). Prepared, sweetened drink mixes are not a substitute for the real thing.

Behind the Scenes–Equipment

Baking pans.   For best results, use only shiny, heavy aluminum pans. *Nonstick pans* are fine to use, provided you're absolutely certain that the finish isn't worn or damaged. If you have any doubts, prepare the pan according to the recipe directions. Each recipe will state the specific type and size pan to use, and I strongly recommend using the pan suggested. If that's not possible, substitute a pan with the same area capacity (see list of pan substitutions, page 25), and adjust the baking time accordingly.

Cake testers.   In the old days, Grandma plucked out a straw from a new broom to test her cakes, and then set it aside just for that purpose. If you're short on new brooms, use a toothpick, a wire cake tester (a thin metal wire with a loop handle at one end), or a 6-inch *wooden* skewer (metal skewers are too thick).

Double boiler.   This consists of two saucepans that fit together, one above the other. The bottom pan is filled one-third with water; the top pan holds ingredients you want melted or cooked. If you don't own a double boiler, improvise by filling a 2-quart saucepan one-third with water, then set a smaller saucepan or heat-resistant mixing bowl snugly into the pan.

Electric mixer.   Unless you have a very strong arm and the ability to beat at the rate of 100 strokes per minute for 6 minutes or longer, I strongly recommend using an electric mixer to make the majority of cakes in this book. I use a heavy-duty stationary stand mixer, but a portable hand mixer will do the job also.

Food processor.   This is not essential, but saves time when chopping and grinding large amounts of nuts, carrots, or dried fruit. When making pastry dough for shortcakes or cobblers, use it to cut the butter into the dry ingredients.

Grater.   Used to remove the peel (colored part of the rind, not the bitter white pith below it) from lemons and oranges, a grater is also good for grating chocolate for decoration.

To grate the peel, first choose fruit that is deep-colored, thick, and firm. Wash and dry the fruit, then rub it across a small section of the grater, using short strokes. If you're using a four-sided grater, choose the side with the smallest holes. Remove the peel with a stiff pastry brush or tap the grater several times against the work surface.

Measuring cups.   You need two types—one to measure liquids, the other to measure dry ingredients. Use a glass or plastic measuring cup with clear markings to measure liquids. For dry ingredients, you need a set of nesting cups (¼ cup, ⅓ cup, ½ cup, and 1 cup) that have flat rims.

Measuring spoons.   These are sold in nesting sets of ⅛ teaspoon, ¼ teaspoon, ½ teaspoon, 1 teaspoon, and 1 tablespoon.

Oven.   This is the most important piece of cake-making equipment you own. Use a mercury oven thermometer to monitor the thermostat and have the oven calibrated if the temperature is 50°F off in either direction.

Pastry blender.   This is used for cutting butter into dry ingredients or for mashing ripe bananas. Choose one with flat, inflexible steel blades rather than one with thin wires—it's sturdier.

Pastry brushes.   Use good-quality brushes ½ to 1 inch wide. They're great for spreading hot glaze on cakes, removing grated peel from between the holes of the grater, and brushing away unwanted confectioners' sugar or cake crumbs from the serving platter.

Serrated knife.   This type of knife is used to slice angel food cake, sponge cake, and chiffon cake.

Sifter.   I use the old-fashioned kind with a hand crank because it works well and I'm sentimental about things that are old. A single-screen sifter with a squeeze handle is good also, and some bakers prefer a triple-screen sifter (the flour passes through three mesh screens, thereby being sifted three times with one action). In lieu of any of the above, a 6-inch-wide strainer with a stainless steel or nylon mesh screen is fine, too.

Spatulas.   Rubber spatulas are indispensable for mixing and folding, scraping the bowl, and smoothing the batter. I own several in various sizes, but the one I use most often has a 4-inch head and is 16 inches from top to bottom. For spreading fillings and frostings, I use an 8-inch-long, 1½-inch-wide, thin-bladed metal spatula.

Strainer.   I use a small, fine-meshed strainer for sifting small amounts of dry ingredients or for straining freshly squeezed lemon or orange juice. (See **Sifter** for further discussion.)

Thermometer.   Don't bake without it! A mercury oven thermometer ensures that a cake is baking at the appropriate temperature. Put it in the center of the oven when you preheat, and wait 15 minutes before checking the temperature. If it's 50°F above or below the temperature you set, it's time to have the oven calibrated. In the meantime, adjust the dial and wait until the correct temperature is recorded on the thermometer before putting the cake in the oven.

Timer.   This is good to have, but not essential. If you don't use one, at least write down the time the cake went into the oven. If you do use one, make sure it's accurate—then write down the time the cake went in the oven anyway, just in case.

Wire racks.   Except for angel food and chiffon cakes, every cake must be cooled on a wire rack. Buy at least three cake-layer-sized racks with wire feet that are at least half an inch high to allow plenty of space for air to circulate below the cake. The more air circulating under the cake, the better.

Wire whisk.   This is used to mix together and aerate dry ingredients. A medium-sized whisk is fine.

Techniques: How To Create a Perfect Cake Every Time

Baking a cake from a recipe is easy when you know exactly what each term means. The following alphabetical list describes all of the techniques used in this book.

Preparation Techniques

Adding sugar in several additions until light and fluffy. This means to add sugar to creamed butter, a few tablespoons at a time, beating about 1 minute with an electric mixer after each addition, until the sugar dissolves, the mixture no longer feels grainy, and the mixture turns almost white. (Some recipes, such as Chocolate Fudge Cake, page 57, have a higher proportion of sugar than butter; the graininess will remain even after creaming as directed above—that's okay.)

Alternately stirring in dry ingredients and liquid, beginning and ending with dry ingredients, and blending well after each addition. The best way to do this is with a large rubber spatula or wooden spoon, since an electric mixer can overmix the batter at this point. Using a measuring cup, scoop up about one fourth of the dry ingredients and distribute over the creamed mixture. Gently move the spatula in a circular pattern through the batter, turning the bowl occasionally as you blend ingredients together. Stir only until dry ingredients have been incorporated, scraping bottom and sides of bowl often. Pour in one third of the liquid, and stir just until blended. Repeat procedure, alternating dry and liquid ingredients, and always adding dry ingredients last (this helps bind the mixture together).

Beating. Beating means to mix ingredients rapidly with the intent of forming and trapping air bubbles while producing a smooth mixture. An electric mixer does the job best.

Beating egg whites until they stand in stiff, moist, shiny peaks. For best results, crack and separate eggs when cold, but allow whites to warm to room temperature before beating to achieve better volume. Using electric beaters, beat whites on low speed until foamy, then increase speed to medium and add cream of tartar. Watching carefully, beat *just* until whites begin to form stiff peaks. To test, lift the beaters out—if the peaks droop over slightly at the top, but are still moist and shiny, they have been beaten enough.

Beating egg yolks until thick and lemon-colored. Yolks will beat to a greater volume if they're warmed to room temperature first. Beat with electric mixer on high speed until they have increased in volume and turn pale yellow. This will take between 3 and 8 minutes, depending on how many yolks are being beaten. Do not underbeat.

Blending. Blending means to mix ingredients together using a spatula or large spoon, just until smooth and thoroughly combined. This is different from beating because it's a slower, gentler motion. Overmixing will produce a heavy, dense cake with large holes throughout the finished product.

Creaming until light and smooth. Softened butter is mashed until it's pale in color, and smooth and light in texture. If your electric mixer has a paddle attachment, now's the time to use it. Otherwise, beaters are best.

Cutting butter into dry ingredients. For best results, lay pats of cold butter over dry ingredients and, using a pastry blender or two knives, cut through the mixture to form small particles of fat and flour that resemble coarse crumbs or cornmeal.

Folding in egg whites. This means to incorporate beaten egg whites into the batter without breaking down the structure of either. To do this efficiently, use a large rubber spatula and the largest mixing bowl you own. Place about one third of the whites on the batter, then pull the spatula down through the center of the batter. Move spatula under batter, and lift batter that clings to spatula over whites as you pull it out of the mixture. Turn bowl counterclockwise as you work, and scrape bottom and sides of bowl often. Continue to fold in whites until you can barely see them in batter; add remaining whites and repeat procedure until they are fully incorporated.

Kneading. Shortcakes are made with a biscuit dough, which requires kneading. To knead, take dough in your hands and form a ball. Place dough on a lightly floured work surface, then put the palm of your hand in the center of the ball and push dough away from you, stretching it out flat against work surface. Fold stretched dough back over remaining dough, then lift and rotate dough one-quarter turn to the left. Repeat procedure several times until dough is smooth and pliable.

Lining round pans with waxed paper. *To line a round pan with waxed paper,* first cut a sheet of waxed paper slightly larger than the pan. Place pan on paper and draw a circle around pan, using pan as a guide. Remove pan and cut out circle. To cut several liners at once, cut sheets of waxed paper, stack and staple corners together; proceed as described above.

To line a jelly-roll pan, first grease it lightly, then cut a piece of waxed paper about 4 inches longer than the pan. Center paper on pan, short ends extending 2 inches beyond pan. Press paper smoothly onto bottom and sides of pan, folding over excess.

Measuring butter. Each recipe calls for cups or tablespoons of butter. One stick of butter is equivalent to ½ cup butter; 1½ sticks are equivalent to ¾ cup butter; 2 sticks are equivalent to 1 cup butter. Each stick of butter is equivalent to 8 tablespoons.

Measuring dry ingredients. Use a set of standard, graduated measuring cups (see page 10) to measure flour, sugar, oats, large amounts of cocoa, and other dry ingredients. Use graduated measuring spoons (see page 10) to measure baking powder, baking soda, spices, cream of tartar, small amounts of cocoa powder, and other dry ingredients.

To measure flour: Unless otherwise stated, flour does not have to be sifted. Instead, with a wire whisk or fork, stir flour several times in its container to aerate. Spoon it lightly into measuring cup until it overflows, then level top with edge of a metal spatula or knife. If you pack, tap, or shake measuring cup, you *will not* get an accurate measurement.

To measure granulated sugar: Spoon or scoop sugar into measuring cup and level with edge of metal spatula or knife. If sugar is lumpy, break up lumps with your fingertips or push sugar through a fine-meshed strainer before measuring.

To measure brown sugar: Spoon into measuring cup, pressing down firmly until cup is filled to the rim, then level with edge of metal spatula or knife.

To measure cocoa: Spoon *unsifted* cocoa directly into measuring cup, then level with edge of metal spatula or knife. If recipe calls for sifted cocoa powder, sift powder onto a sheet of waxed paper, then spoon lightly into measuring cup and level with edge of metal spatula or knife.

To measure confectioners' sugar: Whisk, stir, or sift confectioners' sugar to remove lumps; spoon or pour it into a measuring cup, and level it with edge of metal spatula or knife.

Measuring liquid ingredients. Use glass or plastic measuring cups with clear markings and a pouring spout. They're sold in several sizes, and it's handy to own the 1- and 2-cup sizes. To measure accurately, put cup on a flat work surface; bend down so your eye is at cup level, and fill cup to correct mark.

Melting chocolate.   Unless otherwise directed, melt chocolate in the top part of a double boiler over hot—not simmering—water, stirring occasionally until smooth. Be sure pan is dry before you add chocolate—one drop of water will tighten chocolate and make it impossible to work with. If this happens, add ½ teaspoon solid vegetable shortening (not butter or oil) for every 1 ounce of chocolate, and stir until chocolate is smooth and glossy again.

Separating eggs.   Eggs separate more easily when they are cold. You need three bowls: one for the whites, another for the yolks, and a third as a safety net. If you break the yolk when cracking the shell, just let the whole egg fall into the third bowl and save it for some other use.

To separate yolks from whites, first tap side of egg firmly on the edge of a bowl to crack the shell. Using both hands, separate the two halves of the shell, letting some of the white run out into a bowl. Pour yolk back and forth from one half of the shell to the other, letting all of the white run out. Drop yolk into second bowl. Always separate the white into an empty bowl to prevent any future broken yolks from spoiling the whole lot. If a drop of yolk falls into the white, remove it with the corner of a paper towel or the tip of a cracked shell.

Sifting.   Here's the scoop: Unless specifically stated, you don't have to sift flour or other dry ingredients. Instead, aerate flour in its container by vigorously stirring it with a wire whisk or fork before measuring. After measuring and combining flour with other dry ingredients, whisk or stir them together to aerate further and to distribute ingredients evenly throughout.

When a recipe calls for sifting dry ingredients, sift *before* measuring. Place the measuring cup on a piece of waxed paper, and sift directly over cup until it overflows. Level top with edge of metal spatula or knife, without tapping or shaking cup. The flour that falls on the waxed paper may be returned to its container.

Baking Techniques

Before baking a cake, make sure the oven is preheated and the rack(s) positioned according to the recipe. Once the batter is completely mixed, bake the cake immediately, following the guidelines below for baking, testing, and cooling the cake.

Filling the pan.   Pour batter into prepared pan, using a rubber spatula to scrape the bottom and sides of bowl. Push some of the batter up against the sides of pan, or twirl pan in one direction until some of the batter clings to sides of pan. This will help batter rise evenly. If pan is square or rectangular, be sure to push some of the batter into the corners. No matter what type of pan you're using, always spread batter toward sides of pan and smooth the top. Too much batter in the center will produce a lopsided cake. If you're filling more than one pan, use a 1-cup measurer to alternately divide the batter between the pans. *Note:* See **Substituting Pan Size** (page 24) if you are using a pan other than the one called for in the recipe.

Placing the pans in the oven. Place filled pan in center of designated rack, close oven door, and *do not open it again* until 5 or 10 minutes before the conclusion of the suggested baking time. If you're baking two or more pans simultaneously, stagger them on racks, keeping them about 2 inches away from sides and back of oven. Pans lying side by side in the oven should not touch so that hot air always circulates freely around pans.

Testing the cake for doneness. Each recipe specifies how long to bake the cake; but since every oven bakes differently, it's best to start testing about 5 minutes before the given time. To test, gently insert a toothpick or wire cake tester into center of cake. If cake is done, tester will be clean and dry when you withdraw it. If a few dry crumbs are on tester, cake needs another minute or two. If heavy, wet batter clings to tester, cake needs another 5 to 10 minutes. Other signs that the cake is done: Surface of cake looks dry and cake springs back when gently pressed in the center. Some bakers advise waiting for cake to retract from sides of pan, but at that point you run the risk of overbaking the cake.

> "Always be careful in taking the cake from the oven. Put your ear to it, if you hear it tick you will know it is not done."
>
> —*Consolidated Library of Modern Cooking and Household Recipes, Vol. III.,*
> *R. J. Bodmer Company, 1904*

Cooling the cake. When cake tests done, immediately place pan on a wire rack. Unless otherwise stated, cool for 10 minutes before loosening edges with a metal spatula or the tip of a sharp knife. Cover cake with an inverted rack; flip both over and remove pan. The cake is now wrong side up. Cover cake with another inverted rack and flip right side up to cool completely. (If cake fails to drop out of pan, don't attempt to coax it from pan. Turn it right side up and cool on rack another 5 minutes.) Generally speaking, layer cakes will cool within 1 hour, 10-inch tube cakes and 9-inch loaf cakes within 2 hours.

Angel food and chiffon cakes are cooled in the pan. After baking, invert immediately onto a funnel or use two or three small cans to prop up the pan. When the cake is cool (about 2 hours), run a long, thin knife between cake and pan to loosen.

 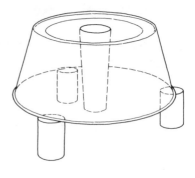

Inverting an angel food cake pan using a metal funnel

Inverting an angel food cake pan by propping it on three small cans

Filling and Frosting Techniques

Any fresh, moist cake may be eaten plain, dusted with confectioners' sugar, or glazed with a thin icing. Layer cakes are particularly luscious when filled and frosted. Each recipe offers suggestions on finishing the cake, but don't feel compelled to stick with the suggestions. If you prefer, make your own choices from "Frostings, Fillings, and Glazes." For example, you might want to glaze a cake instead of dusting it with confectioners' sugar, or substitute a filling or frosting with another. Whatever you decide, don't be afraid to experiment—you might create a new classic!

Amounts of filling and frosting to use. Apply fillings and frostings generously—an 8- or 9-inch, two- or three-layer cake requires ¾ to 1 cup filling between layers and 1½ to 2 cups frosting for the top and sides.

Filling and frosting the cake. Before filling and frosting the cake, it helps to freeze the *cooled* cake for 30 minutes to prevent loose crumbs from seeping through the frosting and spoiling the appearance of the cake. As an alternative, applying a glaze of warm, thinned apricot jam to the top and sides of the cake (see page 146) works well too, and tastes delicious as well. Just be sure to

18

Adding the filling for a two-layer cake to the right-side-up first layer, which sits on an inverted cake pan

Using a metal spatula to spread frosting on cooled top and sides of cake—first with a thin layer, then with a larger amount once first layer has set

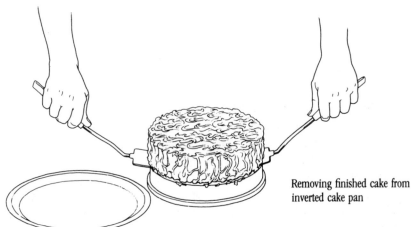

Removing finished cake from inverted cake pan

allow the glaze to set before filling and frosting the cake. If you lack the time or the glaze, brushing off crumbs with a pastry brush before you start also helps.

If cake is lopsided, trim off excess with a sharp serrated knife, making the top as level as possible. (Freezing cake first makes this easier.)

Before filling or frosting cake, put it on an inverted cake pan that is the same size, or slightly smaller, than the cake. This allows you to turn cake easily while frosting, and keeps the serving platter free of unwanted frosting.

To frost a two-layer cake, place one layer right side up on the inverted pan. Using a metal spatula, spread top evenly with about ¾ to 1 cup filling. Gently place second layer wrong side up on first layer (so that tops are together). Spread a thin layer of frosting around sides and over top of cake (this helps to seal in crumbs, too), rotating pan as you apply frosting. Allow frosting to set about 5 minutes. Heap a larger amount of frosting over sides, smoothing or swirling it with the spatula so that sides are covered completely. Smooth or swirl remaining frosting over top of cake. Slip two long metal spatulas under cake; carefully lift and slide onto serving platter.

To frost a three-layer cake, place first layer wrong side up and spread with ¾ to 1 cup filling. Place next layer right side up and repeat. Place third layer wrong side up and proceed with directions for two-layer cake.

Final Touches

You don't have to be an expert with a pastry bag to produce a great-looking cake. Simple cake decorations often make the prettiest presentations. The following list offers a wide range of easy, mostly edible decorations you can apply to almost any cake.

Candied ginger, oranges, and glacé cherries.

Candied orange peel.   Remove colored peel only (not white pith below) from 1 orange; cut into strips ⅛ inch wide and 1½ inches long. Simmer peel in ⅓ cup light corn syrup for 5 minutes, stirring frequently until peel turns deep orange and curls slightly. Lift peel from syrup and spread on lightly oiled aluminum foil to cool.

Chocolate curls.   Melt four 1-ounce squares semisweet chocolate and 1 tablespoon solid vegetable shortening in top of double boiler, stirring frequently until smooth. Transfer to a small, square container and freeze 30 minutes until firm. Remove chocolate from container; scrape across surface with cheese slicer or vegetable peeler to make curls.

Chocolate drizzle.   Chop 1 square semisweet chocolate; place in small plastic bag with 1 teaspoon butter. Seal bag; place in bowl of hot water until chocolate and butter melt. Remove bag from water; dry with paper towels. Open bag; stir mixture together with small spoon to combine, then seal bag. Cut tip off one corner of bottom of bag; squeeze bag to form thin stream of melted chocolate. Drizzle around top edge of frosted cake, letting chocolate run down sides.

Chocolate shavings.   Grate squares of semisweet chocolate on largest hole of hand grater.

Fresh fruit.   Strawberries, whole and unhulled, plain or dipped into chocolate (see page 158); other berries, cherries, grapes, sliced bananas, and kiwifruit. Sprigs of fresh mint arranged alongside the fruit create a pretty effect, too.

Fresh, unsprayed flowers.

Jelly beans, sprinkles, small colored candies, or chocolate chips.

Small macaroons, amaretti, or mint cookies.

Toasted chopped nuts.   Sprinkle on top of cake or press into sides of cake (see next entry).

Toasted flaked coconut.   To toast flaked coconut or shelled nuts, position rack in center of oven; preheat to 350°F. Place flaked coconut or shelled, whole nuts on an ungreased baking pan large enough to hold them in one layer. Toast 15 to 20 minutes, or until lightly browned, stirring occasionally.

Whole nuts.   Including pistachios, almonds, macadamias, and hazelnuts; pecan and walnut halves.

Cutting the Cake

Angel food, sponge, and chiffon cakes.   Use a sharp, serrated knife and cut with a sawing motion. Or use two forks (one in each hand, tines pressed into cake) and gently press through cake, while pulling forks away from slice, until cake breaks away.

Fruitcakes.   Fruitcakes cut best when chilled. Use a thin, sharp knife and cut with a sawing motion into very thin slices.

Pound cakes, loaf cakes, and tube cakes.   Use a thin, sharp knife and cut with a sawing motion.

Round layer cakes and cheesecakes.   These cakes are usually cut into wedge-shaped pieces. Before cutting, score cake into four equal parts. Insert point of a sharp, thin-bladed knife into center of cake and, with the point down and the handle up, slice cake, pulling knife toward you (see illustration, page 22). Rinse knife in warm water or wipe with a damp cloth after each cut to remove any clinging crumbs or frosting. A cake or pie server with a triangular blade removes each slice easily.

Sheet cakes and square cakes.   Use a thin, sharp knife and cut into small square or rectangular pieces with an up-and-down motion.

Cutting a round cake, which has been scored into four equal parts, using a freshly cleaned, thin-bladed knife

Repeat Performances—
Storing and Freezing Cakes

Wrap and store cakes as described below to prolong freshness. You might enjoy eating them even more on the third or fourth day than you did on the first! Just remember to cool the cakes completely before wrapping.

Frosted cakes will keep in the freezer for one to two months; unfrosted cakes up to three months.

To keep a cut cake fresh, press plastic wrap onto the exposed surface before storing in a cake preserver or additional plastic. (Grandma's trick works, too: Include an apple slice or piece of fresh bread with the cake before wrapping and storing.)

Angel food, chiffon, and sponge cakes. Store at room temperature in a cake preserver or wrapped in several layers of plastic. For freezer storage, wrap snugly in several layers of plastic and one layer of aluminum foil, then label and date. To defrost, remove foil and refrigerate overnight or let stand at room temperature for several hours.

Cakes frosted or filled with whipped cream or custard fillings. These must be kept in the refrigerator. Store in a cake preserver or on a platter covered with a large inverted bowl. Or insert toothpicks and wrap with plastic to form a tent. Do not freeze.

Cakes frosted with buttercream or fudge frosting. To store at room temperature for a few hours, place in a cake preserver or on a platter covered with a large inverted bowl. Or insert toothpicks and wrap with plastic to form a tent. Refrigerate for longer storage, and serve at room temperature. For freezer storage, chill *uncovered* in freezer until firm, then wrap snugly in several layers of plastic and one layer of aluminum foil. Label and date cake before freezing. Defrost *unwrapped* in the refrigerator overnight or at room temperature for several hours.

Cakes frosted with 7-Minute Frosting (page 140) or other egg-white frostings. These must be stored at room temperature since the frosting will separate and fall apart if refrigerated. Store in a cake preserver or on a platter covered with a large inverted bowl. Or insert toothpicks and wrap with plastic to form a tent. Eat as soon as possible.

Cheesecakes. These must be stored in the refrigerator. Cover snugly and serve at room temperature. For freezer storage, chill uncovered in freezer until firm, then wrap in plastic and aluminum foil and return to freezer.

Cupcakes. Most may be stored at room temperature in a tightly sealed plastic bag; Black Bottom Cupcakes (page 104) and frosted cupcakes should be refrigerated. For freezer storage, wrap individually in a layer of plastic and then in aluminum foil. Freeze in large plastic bags, four or five cupcakes to a bag.

Pound cakes, fruitcakes, loaf cakes, and tube cakes. To store at room temperature, wrap in several layers of plastic or place in a cake preserver. For freezer storage, wrap snugly in plastic and then aluminum foil, then label and date. To defrost, remove foil and refrigerate overnight or let stand at room temperature for several hours.

Shortcakes. Refrigerate, do not freeze.

Unfrosted layers. Snugly wrapped in several layers of plastic and one layer of aluminum foil, layers may be kept at room temperature for several days. For freezer storage, wrap as described above, then label and date. To defrost, remove foil and refrigerate overnight or at room temperature for several hours.

On the Road—Mailing and Transporting Cakes

Almost any unfrosted cake will survive the bumpy trail of the postal system if wrapped snugly in several layers of plastic and aluminum foil and placed in a box large enough to hold the cake as well as some packing material. (A shoe box works well for loaf cakes and cupcakes; check a local bakery or five-and-dime for larger boxes.) Wedge crumbled newspapers, paper towels, small Styrofoam bits, or plastic bubble wrap between all sides of the cake and box. Filled or frosted cakes and cheesecakes should not be mailed.

To transport a frosted cake short distances, freeze until firm and then wrap in plastic. Be sure to unwrap cake before it defrosts.

Stand Ins—Substituting Ingredients and Pan Size

Substituting ingredients. These recipes have been tested *as written*, and I strongly suggest baking them that way for best results. They are not written in stone, however, and in some instances changes may be made without drastically altering the results. For example, if the recipe calls for walnuts and you have pecans, go ahead and use them. Likewise for dark and light brown sugar or dark and golden raisins. If you lack an ingredient and want to make a substitution, first check the explanation for the ingredient you want substituted (pages 3 through 7) before making the change. If a substitution is recommended, the recipe will say so; if not, *do not make substitutions.*

Substituting pan size. This is a little trickier, and therefore I strongly urge you to use the size and type of pan stated in the recipe. If that's not possible, you may, with caution, substitute another pan with approximately the same area capacity (number of square inches) as the pan stated in the recipe. For instance, if a recipe specifies a 9-inch-square pan (80 square inches), you can substitute an 8- by 10- by 2-inch oblong pan (80 square inches). Substituting pans with drastically different depths, however, is not recommended—they don't always work.

When necessary, consult the table below for comparative pan sizes. Pans are measured across the top between the inside edges and filled no more than ½ to ⅔ full (tube and loaf pans may be filled slightly higher). Leftover batter may be baked in cupcake tins. Depending on the size and shape of the pan, the cake may need more or less time than specified; start testing at least 5 minutes before the given time.

ROUND CAKE PANS

8 × 1½ inches . . . . 50 square inches
9 × 1½ inches . . . . 64 square inches
8 × 2 inches . . . . 50 square inches
10 × 2 inches . . . . 79 square inches
12 × 2 inches . . . . 113 square inches

SQUARE AND RECTANGULAR PANS

6 × 3 × 2¼ inches . . . . 18 square inches
8 × 8 × 1½ inches . . . . 64 square inches
8 × 10 × 2 inches . . . . 80 square inches
8½ × 4½ × 2½ inches . . . . 38 square inches
9 × 5 × 2¾ inches . . . . 45 square inches
9 × 9 × 1½ inches . . . . 81 square inches
9 × 13 × 2 inches . . . . 117 square inches
10 × 15 × 2 inches . . . . 150 square inches
10½ × 15½ inches × 1 inches . . . . 163 square inches
11 × 4½ × 2¾ inches . . . . 50 square inches
11 × 7 × 1½ inches . . . . 77 square inches
11 × 17 × 1 inches . . . . 187 square inches
11 × 18 × 1 inches . . . . 198 square inches

A 10- by 4-inch tube pan and a 12-cup bundt pan may be used interchangeably, or substitute two 9- by 5¼- by 2¾-inch pans.

TEN BAKING BASICS

1. Read the recipe all the way through before you begin mixing the cake.

2. Use the freshest, finest-quality ingredients available, and allow chilled ingredients to warm to room temperature (about 70°F) before using.

3. Assemble ingredients and measure them accurately, using graduated dry measuring cups for dry ingredients and liquid measuring cups for liquids. Organize ingredients so that they are in the order called for in the recipe.

4. Chop nuts, melt chocolate, beat or separate eggs, and complete any other small tasks stated in the list of ingredients before you mix the cake.

5. Preheat the oven at least 15 minutes before you plan to bake the cake, positioning the oven rack(s) as directed in the recipe, and using an oven thermometer to verify the temperature.

6. Use the right pan size and prepare it for baking according to the recipe directions.

7. Follow recipe directions *exactly* and in the sequence stated.

8. Once dry ingredients have been added, mix the batter just until dry ingredients have been incorporated. Overmixing will decrease volume and create tunnels or uneven texture in cakes.

9. Start checking for doneness about 5 minutes before the time indicated in the recipe to avoid overbaking.

10. Cool cakes completely before wrapping, storing, filling, or frosting.

Layer Cakes

White Layer Cake

2⅔ cups sifted cake flour
3 teaspoons baking powder
½ teaspoon salt
¾ cup butter, softened
1½ cups granulated sugar
5 egg yolks

1 teaspoon vanilla extract
1 cup milk
5 egg whites
½ teaspoon cream of tartar
7-Minute Frosting (page 140)

1.   Position rack in center of oven; preheat to 350°F. Grease two 9-inch round cake pans; line with waxed paper; grease; dust with flour.

2.   On a sheet of waxed paper, sift together flour, baking powder, and salt; set aside.

3.   In a large bowl, and using electric beaters, cream butter until light and smooth. Add sugar in several additions, beating until mixture is light and fluffy. Gradually add egg yolks, beating until mixture has the consistency of lightly whipped cream. Stir in vanilla.

4.   Using a large rubber spatula, alternately stir in dry ingredients and milk, beginning and ending with dry ingredients, and blending well after each addition.

5.   In a separate bowl, and using clean beaters, beat whites until frothy; add cream of tartar and beat until whites stand in stiff, moist, shiny peaks. Fold one third of the whites into batter; fold in remaining whites. Pour batter into prepared pans, dividing equally.

6.   Bake 20 to 25 minutes, or until cake tester inserted in center of cakes comes out clean. Remove pans to wire racks, and cool for 10 minutes. Run the tip of a sharp knife between cake and pan to loosen. Invert pans onto other racks; gently peel off waxed paper. Place paper loosely on layers and invert onto other racks; finish cooling on racks.

7.   Fill and frost with 7-Minute Frosting.

Yield: One 9-inch layer cake.

Chocolate Layer Cake

2 cups all-purpose flour
1½ cups granulated sugar
1 teaspoon baking powder
1 teaspoon baking soda
¼ teaspoon salt
2 eggs, lightly beaten
⅓ cup butter, softened

1½ cups sour cream
1½ teaspoons vanilla extract
3 squares (3 ounces) semisweet
   chocolate, melted and cooled
1 cup semisweet chocolate chips
Fast Fudge Frosting (page 148)

CAKE CUE

To decorate a child's birthday cake, press an animal cookie cutter into the icing. Remove the cutter and fill the outline with small colored candies, jelly beans, or chocolate chips.

1. Position rack in center of oven; preheat to 350°F. Greast two 9-inch round cake pans; line with waxed paper; grease; dust with flour.

2. In a medium bowl, whisk or stir together flour, sugar, baking powder, baking soda, and salt; set aside.

3. In a large bowl, and using electric beaters, beat together eggs, butter, sour cream, and vanilla until smooth and well blended; stir in melted chocolate.

4. Using a large rubber spatula, gradually stir in dry ingredients, blending well after each addition. Stir in chocolate chips. Pour batter into prepared pans, dividing equally.

5. Bake 20 to 25 minutes, or until cake tester inserted in center comes out clean. Remove pans to wire racks, and cool for 10 minutes. Run the tip of a sharp knife between cake and pan to loosen. Invert pans onto other racks; gently peel off waxed paper. Place paper loosely on layers and invert onto other racks; finish cooling on racks.

6. Fill and frost with Fast Fudge Frosting.

Yield: One 9-inch layer cake.

Yellow Layer Cake

A basic cake that never fails.

2⅓ cups sifted cake flour
3 teaspoons baking powder
¼ teaspoon salt
½ cup butter, softened
1¼ cups granulated sugar
2 eggs, lightly beaten

2 teaspoons vanilla extract
½ cup milk
½ cup thick raspberry jam
Basic Buttercream Frosting
(page 142)

1.   Position rack in center of oven; preheat to 350°F. Grease two 9-inch round cake pans; dust with flour.

2.   In a medium bowl, sift together flour, baking powder, and salt; set aside.

3.   In a large bowl, and using electric beaters, cream butter until light and smooth. Add sugar in several additions, beating until mixture is light and fluffy. Gradually add eggs, beating until mixture has the consistency of lightly whipped cream. Beat in vanilla.

4.   Using a large rubber spatula, alternately stir in dry ingredients and milk, beginning and ending with dry ingredients, and blending well after each addition. Pour batter into prepared pans, dividing equally.

5.   Bake 20 minutes, or until a cake tester inserted in the center comes out clean. Remove pans to wire racks. Cool 10 minutes before loosening cakes from pans with a knife and removing. Finish cooling right side up on racks.

6.   Spread one layer with raspberry jam. Place second layer wrong side up on first layer; frost top and sides with Basic Buttercream Frosting.

Yield: One 9-inch layer cake.

Banana Layer Cake

2 cups all-purpose flour
2½ teaspoons baking powder
½ teaspoon baking soda
½ teaspoon ground cinnamon
¼ teaspoon ground nutmeg
½ teaspoon salt
½ cup butter, softened
1¼ cups granulated sugar

2 eggs, lightly beaten
1 teaspoon vanilla extract
1 cup mashed, ripe bananas
½ cup buttermilk
Coconut Cream Filling (page 143)
7-Minute Frosting (page 140)

CAKE CUE

When a recipe calls for buttermilk, and you don't have any, try this: Warm 1 cup whole milk to room temperature. Place 1 tablespoon freshly squeezed lemon juice in a glass measuring cup, then pour in warmed milk to make 1 cup. Stir the two together and let stand for 10 minutes.

1. Position rack in center of oven; preheat to 350°F. Grease two 9-inch round pans; dust with flour.
2. In a medium bowl, whisk or stir together flour, baking powder, baking soda, cinnamon, nutmeg, and salt.
3. In a large bowl, and using electric beaters, cream butter until light and smooth. Add sugar in several additions, beating until mixture is light and fluffy. Gradually add eggs, beating until mixture has the consistency of lightly whipped cream. Stir in vanilla and mashed bananas.
4. Using a large rubber spatula, alternately stir in dry ingredients and buttermilk, beginning and ending with dry ingredients, and blending well after each addition. Pour batter into prepared pans, dividing equally.
5. Bake 20 to 25 minutes, or until a cake tester inserted in center comes out clean. Remove pans to wire racks. Cool 10 minutes before loosening cakes from pans with a knife and removing. Finish cooling right side up on racks.
6. Place one layer right side up on inverted cake pan; spread Coconut Cream Filling over layer. Place second layer wrong side up; frost sides and top with 7-Minute Frosting. Transfer to serving platter.

Yield: One 9-inch layer cake.

Lady Baltimore Cake

3½ cups sifted cake flour
4 teaspoons baking powder
½ teaspoon salt
1 cup butter, softened
2 cups granulated sugar
4 eggs, lightly beaten

1 teaspoon almond extract
1 teaspoon vanilla extract
1 cup milk
Lady Baltimore Frosting (page 153)
7-Minute Frosting (page 140)

1. Position two racks to divide oven into thirds; preheat to 350°F. Grease three 9-inch round cake pans; line each with waxed paper; grease paper; dust with flour.

2. In a medium bowl, whisk or stir together cake flour, baking powder, and salt; set aside.

3. In a large bowl, and using electric beaters, cream butter until light and smooth. Add sugar in several additions, beating until mixture is light and fluffy. Gradually add eggs, beating until mixture has the consistency of lightly whipped cream. Stir in almond and vanilla extracts.

4. Using a large rubber spatula, alternately stir in dry ingredients and milk, beginning and ending with dry ingredients, and blending well after each addition. Pour batter into prepared pans, dividing equally.

5. Bake 25 minutes, or until cake tester inserted in center comes out clean. Remove pans to wire racks, and cool for 10 minutes. Run the tip of a sharp knife between cake and pan to loosen. Invert pans onto other racks; gently peel off waxed paper. Place paper loosely on layers and invert onto other racks; finish cooling on racks.

6. Place one layer wrong side up on inverted cake pan; spread with one half of Lady Baltimore Filling. Place second layer right side up; spread with remaining filling. Place third layer wrong side up; frost top and sides with 7-Minute Icing. Transfer to serving platter.

Yield: One 9-inch, 3-layer cake.

Boston Cream Pie

Vanilla Cream Filling (page 151)
2 cups sifted cake flour
1 cup sugar
2 teaspoons baking powder
¼ teaspoon salt
⅓ cup butter, softened

⅔ cup milk
3 eggs, lightly beaten
1 teaspoon vanilla extract
Chocolate Glaze (page 149)
Chocolate curls (page 20,
    optional)

CAKE CUE

If you bake with the oven light on, turn it off! You might be creating "hot spots" in the oven, causing the cake to bake unevenly.

1. Make Vanilla Cream Filling.
2. Position rack in center of oven; preheat to 375°F. Grease two 8-inch round cake pans; dust with flour.
3. In a large bowl, and using electric beaters set on low speed, whisk together flour, sugar, baking powder, and salt. Add butter, milk, eggs, and vanilla, beating until mixture is smooth and thoroughly combined (about 3 minutes). Pour batter into prepared pans, dividing equally.
4. Bake 20 minutes, or until cake tester inserted in center comes out clean. Cool pans on wire racks 10 minutes, before loosening layers with a knife and removing; finish cooling on racks.
5. Make Chocolate Glaze.
6. *To assemble cake:* Place one layer wrong side up on serving platter; spread top with vanilla cream filling to within 1 inch of edge. Place second layer right side up; spoon warm Chocolate Glaze over cake, letting it run down the sides. Garnish with chocolate curls, if desired.

Yield: One 8-inch layer cake.

Washington Pie: Omit Vanilla Cream Filling; spread layers with ¾ cup of your favorite thick jam. Dust top of cake with confectioners' sugar.

Robert E. Lee Cake

2¼ cups all-purpose flour
2¼ teaspoons baking powder
¼ teaspoon salt
1 cup butter, softened
1¾ cups granulated sugar
4 egg yolks
2 teaspoons vanilla extract
2 teaspoons each grated orange
    and lemon peels

1 cup milk
4 egg whites
¼ teaspoon cream of tartar
Lemon Filling (page 145)
7-Minute Frosting (page 140)
1½ cups flaked coconut

1. Position two racks to divide oven into thirds; preheat to 350°F. Grease three 9-inch round cake pans; dust with flour.
2. In a medium bowl, whisk or stir together flour, baking powder, and salt; set aside.
3. In a large bowl, and using electric beaters, cream butter until light and smooth. Add 1¼ cups of the sugar in several additions, beating until mixture is light and fluffy. Gradually add egg yolks, beating until mixture has the consistency of lightly whipped cream. Stir in vanilla and fruit peels.
4. Using a large rubber spatula, alternately stir in dry ingredients and milk, beginning and ending with dry ingredients, and blending well after each addition.
5. Beat egg whites until frothy; add cream of tartar, beating until whites begin to hold their shape. Add remaining ½ cup sugar, a few tablespoons at a time, beating until whites stand in stiff, moist, shiny peaks; fold whites into batter. Pour batter into prepared pans, dividing equally.
6. Bake 30 to 35 minutes or until cake tester inserted in center comes out clean. Remove pans to wire racks. Cool 10 minutes before loosening cakes from pans with a knife and removing. Finish cooling right side up on racks.
7. Place one layer wrong side up on inverted cake pan; spread with one half of the Lemon Filling. Place second layer wrong side up; spread with remaining filling. Place third layer right side up; frost sides and top with 7-Minute Frosting. Sprinkle coconut over top and sides of cake.

Yield: One 9-inch, 3-layer cake.

CAKE CUE

Always beat egg whites with grease-free beaters in a grease-free bowl. If the whites contain the smallest speck of fat or yolk, they will not beat to their optimal height.

Lane Cake

A southern classic.

3¼ cups sifted cake flour
3½ teaspoons baking powder
¼ teaspoon salt
1 cup butter, softened
1¾ cups granulated sugar
1 teaspoon vanilla extract

1 cup milk
8 egg whites
½ teaspoon cream of tartar
Lane Filling (page 154)
7-Minute Frosting (page 140)

1. Position racks to divide oven into thirds; preheat to 375°F. Grease three 9-inch round cake pans; line with waxed paper; grease; dust with flour.
2. In a medium bowl, whisk or stir together flour, baking powder, and salt.
3. In a large bowl, and using electric beaters, cream butter until light and smooth. Add sugar in several additions, beating until mixture is light and fluffy. Stir in vanilla.
4. Using a large rubber spatula, alternately stir in dry ingredients and milk, beginning and ending with dry ingredients, and blending well after each addition.
5. In a large bowl, and using clean beaters, beat egg whites until frothy. Add cream of tartar, and beat until whites stand in stiff, moist, shiny peaks. Stir one fourth of the whites into batter to lighten; fold in remaining whites. Pour batter into prepared pans, dividing equally.
6. Bake 20 to 25 minutes, or until cake tester inserted in center comes out clean. Then remove pans to wire racks, and cool for 10 minutes. Run the tip of a sharp knife between cake and pan to loosen. Invert pans onto other racks; gently peel off waxed paper. Place paper loosely on layers and invert onto other racks; finish cooling on racks.
7. Place one layer wrong side up on inverted cake pan; spread with one half of the Lane Filling. Place second layer right side up; spread with remaining filling. Place third layer wrong side up; frost top and sides of cake with 7-Minute Frosting.

Yield: One 9-inch, 3-layer cake.

Black Forest Cake

*2 layers Old-Fashioned Devil's
    Food Cake (page 59), cooled
½ cup kirsch
2 cups cold heavy cream
¼ cup confectioners' sugar*

*1 can (16-ounce) pitted red tart
    cherries, drained
Chocolate curls (page 20)
12 pitted cherries with stems*

1. Wrap each cake layer in plastic and freeze until firm (about 15 minutes). Using a sharp serrated knife, cut each layer horizontally to make four thin layers. Generously brush the cut side of each layer with kirsch.

2. In a deep metal or glass bowl, beat cream and sugar until smooth and thick; set aside 1 cup of the whipped cream. Stir drained cherries into remaining whipped cream.

3. Spread one third of the whipped cream–cherry filling on the bottom half of one layer. Repeat with next two layers. Put the fourth layer on the cake; spread with reserved whipped cream. Decorate center of cake with chocolate curls, and arrange cherries around border.

Yield: One 9-inch round cake.

Spice Cakes, Coffee Cakes, and Pound Cakes

Spicy Applesauce Cake

1 cup chopped raisins
½ cup chopped walnuts
2¼ cups all-purpose flour
2 teaspoons baking soda
1 teaspoon ground cinnamon
½ teaspoon ground cloves
½ teaspoon ground nutmeg
½ teaspoon salt

2 eggs, lightly beaten
¾ cup butter, softened
½ cup granulated sugar
1 cup firmly packed light brown
   sugar
1⅔ cups applesauce
Confectioners' sugar

1.   Position rack in center of oven; preheat to 350°F. Grease a 9- by 13- by 2-inch baking pan; line bottom with aluminum foil, allowing ends of foil to extend about 2 inches over sides of pan; grease; dust with flour.

2.   On a sheet of waxed paper, mix raisins and nuts with 2 teaspoons of the flour; set aside.

3.   In a large bowl, and using electric beaters set on low speed, whisk together remaining flour, baking soda, cinnamon, cloves, nutmeg, and salt until well combined. Add eggs, butter, granulated sugar, brown sugar, and applesauce, beating just to moisten ingredients. Increase speed to medium-high, and beat until batter is smooth and well blended (about 2 minutes). Using a large rubber spatula, stir in raisins and nuts. Pour batter into prepared pan, spreading evenly.

4.   Bake 30 to 35 minutes, or until cake tester inserted in center comes out clean. Remove pan to wire rack; cool cake in pan 15 minutes. Using foil ends as handles, lift cake and place on wire rack to finish cooling. When cake is cool, invert onto large serving platter. Carefully peel off foil, and dust with confectioners' sugar.

Yield: One 9- by 13- by 2-inch cake.

Old-Fashioned Gingerbread

Eat this cake out of hand, warm from the oven, or crown with a scoop of vanilla ice cream and dust with cinnamon.

2¼ cups all-purpose flour
1¼ teaspoons baking soda
½ teaspoon salt
1½ teaspoons ground ginger
1 teaspoon ground cinnamon
¼ teaspoon ground cloves

1 cup buttermilk
½ cup butter, softened
2 eggs, lightly beaten
¾ cup firmly packed dark brown sugar
½ cup molasses

~~ ~
CAKE CUE

Honey or molasses will slide out easily from a measuring cup if you oil the cup first.

1. Position rack in center of oven; preheat to 350°F. Grease a 9-inch square baking pan; dust with flour.

2. In a large bowl, and using electric beaters set on low speed, whisk together flour, baking soda, salt, ginger, cinnamon, and cloves. Add buttermilk, butter, eggs, brown sugar, and molasses; beat on low speed just to moisten ingredients. Increase speed to medium-high and beat until mixture is smooth and well combined (about 1 minute). Pour batter into prepared pan, spreading evenly.

3. Bake 25 to 30 minutes, or until cake tester inserted in center comes out clean. Remove pan to wire rack. Cool 15 minutes before cutting in squares and serving.

Yield: One 9-inch square cake.

Pioneer Potato Cake

This cake is moist and spicy, and freezes well.

1¾ cups all-purpose flour
4 tablespoons unsweetened cocoa
   powder
3 teaspoons baking powder
½ teaspoon baking soda
½ teaspoon salt
1 teaspoon ground nutmeg
1 teaspoon ground cinnamon

½ teaspoon ground cloves
1 cup chopped walnuts
¾ cup butter, softened
1¾ cups granulated sugar
3 eggs, lightly beaten
1 cup warm mashed potatoes
¾ cup buttermilk
2 teaspoons grated orange peel

1.   Position rack in center of oven; preheat to 350°F. Grease two 9- by 5- by 2¾-inch loaf pans; dust with flour.

2.   In a small bowl, whisk or stir together flour, cocoa powder, baking powder, baking soda, salt, nutmeg, cinnamon, and cloves. On a sheet of waxed paper, mix walnuts with 2 teaspoons of the dry ingredients; set aside.

3.   In a large bowl, and using electric beaters, cream butter until light and smooth. Add sugar in several additions, beating until mixture is light and fluffy. Gradually add eggs, beating until mixture has the consistency of lightly whipped cream. Stir in warm potatoes.

4.   Using a large rubber spatula, alternately stir in dry ingredients and buttermilk, beginning and ending with dry ingredients, and blending well after each addition. Stir in walnuts and orange peel. Pour batter into prepared pans, dividing equally.

5.   Bake 45 minutes, or until cake tester inserted in center comes out clean. Remove pans to wire racks. Cool 10 minutes before loosening cakes from pans with a knife and removing. Finish cooling right side up on racks.

Yield: Two 9- by 5- by 2¾-inch loaves.

Pumpkin Cake with Gingered Whipped Cream

2 cups all-purpose flour
3 teaspoons baking powder
¼ teaspoon baking soda
½ teaspoon salt
1 teaspoon ground cinnamon
¼ teaspoon ground cloves
⅛ teaspoon ground nutmeg
½ cup butter, softened
¾ cup firmly packed dark brown
    sugar

2 eggs, lightly beaten
3 tablespoons molasses
¾ cup canned pumpkin
1 teaspoon vanilla extract
⅓ cup buttermilk
Gingered Whipped Cream (recipe
    follows)

1.   Position rack in center of oven; preheat to 350°F. Grease a 9- by 13- by 2-inch baking pan; line bottom with aluminum foil, allowing ends of foil to extend about 2 inches over sides of pan; grease; dust with flour.

2.   In a medium bowl, whisk or stir together flour, baking powder, baking soda, salt, cinnamon, cloves, and nutmeg; set aside.

3.   In a large bowl, and using electric beaters, cream butter until light and smooth. Add sugar in several additions, beating until mixture is light and fluffy. Gradually add eggs, beating until mixture has the consistency of lightly whipped cream. Stir in molasses, pumpkin, and vanilla.

4.   Using a large rubber spatula, alternately stir in dry ingredients and buttermilk, beginning and ending with dry ingredients, and blending well after each addition. Pour batter into prepared pan, spreading evenly.

5.   Bake 25 minutes, or until cake tester inserted in center comes out clean. Remove pan to wire rack; cool cake in pan 15 minutes. Using foil ends as handles, lift cake and place on wire rack to finish cooling. When cake is cool, invert onto large serving platter. Carefully peel off foil.

6.   Prepare Gingered Whipped Cream. Spread over cooled cake just before serving.

Yield: One 9- by 13- by 2-inch cake.

Gingered Whipped Cream

1 cup chilled heavy cream
1 teaspoon finely chopped
  crystallized ginger

In a deep metal or glass bowl, and using electric beaters, beat cream until thick; fold in crystallized ginger.

Yield: 2 cups.

Spice 1-2-3-4 Cake

In colonial days, women remembered this recipe by its ingredients: 1 cup butter, 2 cups sugar, 3 cups flour, and 4 eggs. My family has renamed it the 1-2-3-4 cake, because that's how quickly it's eaten!

3 cups sifted cake flour
1 tablespoon baking powder
2 teaspoons unsweetened cocoa
  powder
½ teaspoon ground cloves
¼ teaspoon ground allspice
½ teaspoon ground nutmeg

1½ teaspoons ground cinnamon
1 cup butter, softened
2 cups granulated sugar
4 eggs, lightly beaten
2 tablespoons molasses
1 cup milk or orange juice
Confectioners' sugar (optional)

1.   Position rack in lower third of oven; preheat to 350°F. Grease a 10- by 4-inch tube or a 12-cup bundt pan; dust with flour.

2.   In a medium bowl, sift together cake flour, baking powder, cocoa powder, cloves, allspice, nutmeg, and cinnamon; set aside.

3.   In a large bowl, and using electric beaters, cream butter until light and smooth. Add sugar in several additions, beating until mixture is light and fluffy. Gradually add eggs, beating until mixture has the consistency of lightly whipped cream. Stir in molasses.

4.   Using a large rubber spatula, alternately stir in dry ingredients and milk, beginning and ending with dry ingredients, and blending well after each addition. Pour batter into prepared pan, spreading evenly.

5.   Bake 55 to 60 minutes, or until cake tester inserted in center comes out clean. Remove pan to wire rack. Cool 10 minutes before loosening cake from pan with a knife and removing. Finish cooling right side up on rack. Serve plain or dust with confectioners' sugar.

Yield: One 10-inch tube cake.

Original 1-2-3-4 Cake: Omit spices and molasses. Add 1 teaspoon vanilla extract and 2 tablespoons grated orange peel.

CAKE CUE

To make vanilla confectioners' sugar, pour a box of confectioners' sugar into a jar that has a tight-fitting lid. Split one or two vanilla beans lengthwise and push them into the confectioners' sugar; cover and let stand for a few days before using. Replace sugar as needed for up to two months before discarding the beans. Sprinkle over cakes in place of plain confectioners' sugar.

Snickerdoodle

Mixes like a muffin; bakes like a cake.

1 cup plus 1 teaspoon all-purpose
    flour
¾ cup granulated sugar
2 teaspoons baking powder
¼ teaspoon salt
½ teaspoon ground cinnamon
1 egg, lightly beaten
6 tablespoons butter, melted

½ cup milk
½ cup chopped dates
½ cup chopped walnuts
½ cup semisweet chocolate chips
1 tablespoon granulated sugar
    mixed with ½ teaspoon ground
    cinnamon

1.   Position rack in center of oven; preheat to 350°F. Grease an 8- by 8- by 1½-inch square cake pan; dust with flour.

2.   In a medium bowl, whisk or stir together the 1 cup flour, sugar, baking powder, salt, and cinnamon. Make a well in the center; add egg, melted butter, and milk. Using a large rubber spatula, stir mixture until smooth and thoroughly combined.

3.   On a sheet of waxed paper, mix dates and nuts with the 1 teaspoon flour; stir into batter with chocolate chips. Pour batter into prepared pan; sprinkle top evenly with cinnamon-sugar mixture.

4.   Bake 25 minutes, or until cake tester inserted in center comes out clean. Remove pan to wire rack. Cool 15 minutes before cutting in squares and serving.

Yield: One 8-inch square cake.

Chocolate-Almond Swirl Coffeecake

1⅔ cups granulated sugar
1½ teaspoons ground cinnamon
2 cups (one 12-ounce package)
  semisweet chocolate chips
1 cup coarsely chopped almonds
2¾ cups all-purpose flour
2 teaspoons baking powder

½ teaspoon baking soda
½ teaspoon salt
1 cup butter, softened
3 eggs, lightly beaten
½ teaspoon vanilla extract
¼ teaspoon almond extract
1 cup sour cream

1.   Position rack in center of oven; preheat to 350°F. Grease a 12-cup bundt pan or a 10- by 4-inch tube pan; dust with flour.

2.   In a medium bowl, stir together ⅓ cup of the sugar and the cinnamon. Add chocolate chips and almonds; stir to combine and set aside.

3.   In a separate bowl, whisk or stir together flour, baking powder, baking soda, and salt; set aside.

4.   In a large bowl, and using electric beaters, cream butter until light and smooth. Add remaining 1⅓ cups sugar in several additions, beating until mixture is light and fluffy. Gradually add eggs, beating until mixture has the consistency of lightly whipped cream. Beat in vanilla and almond extracts.

5.   Using a large rubber spatula, alternately stir in dry ingredients and sour cream, beginning and ending with dry ingredients, and blending well after each addition. Pour one third of the batter into prepared pan; spread evenly. Sprinkle one third of the chocolate mixture over batter. Pour half of the remaining batter into the pan; spread evenly. Sprinkle half of the remaining chocolate mixture over batter. Pour remaining batter into pan; spread evenly and sprinkle remaining chocolate mixture over top. Cut through batter several times with a thin-bladed knife to marble slightly.

6.   Bake 55 to 60 minutes, or until cake tester inserted in center comes out clean. Remove pan to wire rack. Cool 15 minutes before loosening cake from pan with a knife and removing. Finish cooling right side up on rack.

Yield: One 12-cup bundt cake.

Sour Cream Coffeecake with Apricot Glaze

1½ cups plus 2 tablespoons
  granulated sugar
1 teaspoon ground cinnamon
1 cup coarsely chopped walnuts
2 cups all-purpose flour
1½ teaspoons baking powder
½ teaspoon baking soda
½ teaspoon salt
1 cup butter, softened

2 eggs, lightly beaten
1 teaspoon vanilla extract
1 cup sour cream
⅓ cup apricot preserves
2 tablespoons firmly packed light
  brown sugar
1 teaspoon freshly squeezed
  lemon juice

1. Position rack in lower third of oven; preheat to 350°F. Grease a 12-cup bundt pan or a 10- by 4-inch tube pan; dust with flour.

2. In a small bowl, stir together the 2 tablespoons sugar, the cinnamon, and walnuts; set aside.

3. In a medium bowl, whisk or stir together flour, baking powder, baking soda, and salt; set aside.

4. In a large bowl, and using electric beaters, cream butter until light and smooth. Add the 1½ cups sugar in several additions, beating until mixture is light and fluffy. Gradually add eggs, beating until mixture has the consistency of lightly whipped cream. Stir in dry ingredients. Stir in vanilla and sour cream.

5. Pour half of the batter into prepared pan; spread evenly. Sprinkle half of the nut mixture over batter. Pour remaining batter into pan; spread evenly. Sprinkle remaining nut mixture over top. Cut through batter several times with a thin-bladed knife to marble slightly.

6. Bake 45 to 50 minutes, or until cake tester inserted in center comes out clean. Remove pan to wire rack. Cool 10 minutes before loosening cake from pan with a knife and removing. Finish cooling right side up on rack.

7. Heat apricot preserves and brown sugar in a small, heavy saucepan over low heat; stir frequently until dissolved (about 3 minutes). Remove from heat and stir in lemon juice. Brush glaze over top and sides of warm cake. Cool cake at least 1 hour before serving.

Yield: One 12-cup bundt cake.

Old-Fashioned Yankee Pound Cake

Pound cake is delicious by itself and makes the perfect base for an assortment of other desserts. Serve with fresh fruit and whipped cream; or crown with a scoop of vanilla ice cream and Blueberry Sauce (page 147) or Raspberry-Peach Sauce (page 152). The flavor of this cake improves greatly if cake is wrapped and stored at room temperature for at least 24 hours before slicing.

2¾ cups sifted cake flour
1 teaspoon baking powder
½ teaspoon salt
¼ teaspoon ground mace
1 cup butter, softened

1¼ cups granulated sugar
5 eggs, lightly beaten
2 teaspoons lemon juice
½ teaspoon grated lemon peel

CAKE CUE

In a pinch, make your own cake flour by sifting together 3 parts all-purpose flour with 1 part cornstarch. Store in an airtight container and use whenever cake flour is called for in a recipe. Sift before using.

1. Position rack in center of oven; preheat to 350°F. Grease a 12-cup bundt pan or a 10- by 4-inch tube pan; dust with flour.

2. In a medium bowl, sift together cake flour, baking powder, salt, and mace; set aside.

3. In a large bowl, and using electric beaters, cream butter until light and smooth. Add sugar in several additions, beating until mixture is light and fluffy. Gradually add eggs, beating until mixture has the consistency of lightly whipped cream. *Do not underbeat.* Beat in lemon juice and peel.

4. Sift ¼ cup dry ingredients over creamed mixture; fold gently, but thoroughly. Repeat procedure with remaining dry ingredients. Pour batter into prepared pan, spreading evenly.

5. Bake 50 to 60 minutes, or until cake tester inserted in center comes out clean. Remove pan to wire rack. Cool 10 minutes before loosening cake from pan with a knife and removing. Finish cooling right side up on rack.

Yield: One 12-cup bundt cake.

Marble Pound Cake

The flavor of this cake improves greatly when cake is wrapped and stored at room temperature for at least 24 hours before slicing.

2¾ cups sifted cake flour
1 teaspoon baking powder
½ teaspoon salt
1 cup butter, softened
2 cups granulated sugar

5 eggs, lightly beaten
1 teaspoon vanilla extract
¼ teaspoon almond extract
3 tablespoons unsweetened cocoa
   powder

1. Position rack in center of oven; preheat to 350°F. Grease a 12-cup bundt pan or a 10- by 4-inch tube pan; dust with flour.
2. In a medium bowl, sift together flour, baking powder, and salt; set aside.
3. In a large bowl, and using electric beaters, cream butter until light and smooth. Add sugar in several additions, beating until mixture is light and fluffy. Gradually add eggs, beating until mixture has the consistency of lightly whipped cream. *Do not underbeat.* Beat in vanilla and almond extracts.
4. Sift ¼ cup dry ingredients over batter; fold in gently but thoroughly. Repeat procedure with remaining dry ingredients. Transfer one third of the batter to a small bowl; add cocoa powder, blending well to make chocolate batter. Fill the prepared pan with the batters, alternating large spoonfuls of light batter with small spoonfuls of chocolate batter. Pull a knife through the batter two or three times to create the marbling.
5. Bake 50 to 60 minutes, or until cake tester inserted in center comes out clean. Remove pan to wire rack. Cool 10 minutes before loosening cake from pan with a knife and removing. Finish cooling right side up on rack.

Yield: One 12-cup bundt cake.

Amazing Tunnel Cake

This butter cake has a fudgy center.

¾ cup Chocolate Syrup (recipe
    follows)
2⅔ cups all-purpose flour
2¼ teaspoons baking powder
½ teaspoon salt
1 cup butter, softened
2 cups granulated sugar

4 eggs, lightly beaten
2 teaspoons vanilla extract
1 cup milk
¼ teaspoon baking soda
Chocolate Glaze (page 149,
    optional)
Confectioners' sugar (optional)

1. Make Chocolate Syrup.
2. Position rack in lower third of oven; preheat to 350°F. Grease a 10- by 4-inch tube or 12-cup bundt pan; dust with flour.
3. In a medium bowl, whisk or stir together flour, baking powder, and salt; set aside.
4. In a large bowl, and using electric beaters, cream butter until light and smooth. Add sugar in several additions, beating until mixture is light and fluffy. Slowly pour in beaten eggs, beating until mixture is light, fluffy, and smooth. Beat in vanilla.
5. Using a large rubber spatula, alternately stir in dry ingredients and milk, beginning and ending with dry ingredients, and blending well after each addition. Pour two thirds of the batter into prepared pan, spreading evenly.
6. Add baking soda to Chocolate Syrup; stir thoroughly. Pour Chocolate Syrup into remaining batter, blending thoroughly. Pour chocolate batter over vanilla batter, spreading evenly. *Do not stir batters together.*
7. Bake 50 to 55 minutes, or until cake tester inserted in center comes out clean. Remove pan to wire rack. Cool 10 minutes before loosening cake from pan with a knife and removing. Finish cooling right side up on rack. If desired, pour warm Chocolate Glaze over the cake, letting it run down the sides, or dust with confectioners' sugar.

Yield: One 10- by 4-inch tube cake.

Chocolate Syrup

½ *cup granulated sugar*
½ *cup unsweetened cocoa powder*
¼ *cup light corn syrup*

½ *cup hot tap water*
½ *teaspoon vanilla extract*

Combine sugar, cocoa powder, corn syrup, and the water in a small, heavy saucepan. Cook and stir over low heat until completely blended; simmer 2 minutes, stirring constantly. Remove from heat; stir in vanilla. Cool to room temperature before using.

Yield: About ¾ cup.

Lemon–Poppy Seed Cake

2½ cups all-purpose flour
2¼ teaspoons baking powder
½ teaspoon salt
1 cup butter, softened
1¾ cups granulated sugar
5 eggs, separated
2 teaspoons vanilla extract
⅓ cup freshly squeezed lemon
  juice

⅔ cup milk
½ teaspoon grated lemon peel
⅓ cup poppy seeds
¼ teaspoon cream of tartar
Lemon Glaze (page 139,
  optional)
Confectioners' sugar (optional)

1. Position rack in lower third of oven; preheat to 350°F. Grease a 12-cup bundt pan or a 10- by 4-inch tube pan; dust with flour.
2. In a medium bowl, whisk or stir together flour, baking powder, and salt; set aside.
3. In a large bowl, and using electric beaters, cream butter until light and smooth. Add sugar in several additions, beating until mixture is light and fluffy. Add yolks, one at a time, beating until mixture is light, smooth, and fluffy. Stir vanilla into lemon juice; slowly pour into butter mixture, and beat until blended.
4. Using a large rubber spatula, alternately stir in dry ingredients and milk, beginning and ending with dry ingredients, and blending well after each addition. Stir in peel and poppy seeds.
5. In a separate bowl, and using clean beaters, beat whites until frothy; add cream of tartar and beat until whites stand in stiff, moist, shiny peaks. Fold one third of the whites into batter; fold in remaining whites. Pour batter into prepared pan, spreading evenly.
6. Bake 50 to 55 minutes, or until cake tester inserted in center comes out clean. Remove pan to wire rack. Cool 15 minutes before loosening cake from pan with a knife and removing. Finish cooling right side up on rack. If desired, drizzle Lemon Glaze over cake or dust with confectioners' sugar.

Yield: One 12-cup bundt cake.

Chocolate Cakes

Chocolate Fudge Cake

4 squares (4 ounces) unsweetened
   chocolate
1 tablespoon instant-coffee
   powder
¼ teaspoon salt

2 cups granulated sugar
½ cup butter, softened
3 eggs
1 cup all-purpose flour
Confectioners' sugar

   1.   Position rack in center of oven; preheat to 350°F. Grease an 8-inch springform pan; dust with flour.

   2.   In the top of a double boiler over hot, not boiling, water, combine chocolate, coffee powder, salt, and ½ cup water, stirring often until chocolate melts and mixture is smooth. Add ½ cup of the sugar, stirring about 2 minutes or until sugar dissolves. Remove top part of boiler from water; cool chocolate until warm to the touch.

   3.   In a large bowl, and using electric beaters, cream butter until light and smooth. Gradually add remaining 1½ cups sugar, beating well after each addition. (Mixture will be slightly grainy.) Add eggs, one at a time, beating 1 minute after each addition. Stir in cooled chocolate. Add flour, ¼ cup at a time, blending well after each addition. Pour batter into prepared pan.

   4.   Bake 50 to 55 minutes, or until cake tester inserted in center comes out clean. Remove pan to wire rack, and cool 10 minutes. Run a knife around sides of cake to loosen it from pan. Remove outer rim of pan; finish cooling on rack. Slide a long metal spatula under cake to loosen it from bottom of pan; transfer cake to a serving platter. Dust with confectioners' sugar.

Yield: One 8-inch round cake.

Chocolate-Nut Upside-Down Cake

¼ cup butter
½ cup firmly packed light brown
  sugar
½ cup pure maple syrup
1 tablespoon grated orange peel
1½ cups chopped pecans
3 tablespoons dark or light rum
¼ cup unsweetened cocoa powder
2 cups all-purpose flour

1 teaspoon baking soda
½ teaspoon salt
1½ cups granulated sugar
½ cup butter, softened
1 cup sour cream
1½ teaspoons vanilla extract
3 eggs, lightly beaten
Ice cream (optional)

CAKE CUE

*When you run out
of brown sugar,
make your own by
adding ¼ cup
molasses to ¾ cup
granulated sugar;
mix thoroughly to
make 1 cup firmly
packed brown sugar.*

1.   Position rack in lower third of oven; preheat to 350°F. Grease a 12-cup bundt pan or a 10- by 4-inch tube pan.

2.   In a small saucepan over low heat, melt the ¼ cup butter; remove from heat. Add brown sugar, maple syrup, and orange peel, stirring until well blended. Pour into prepared pan and sprinkle pecans evenly on top; set aside.

3.   In a small bowl, stir rum and cocoa together until smooth; set aside.

4.   In a large bowl, and using electric beaters set on low speed, whisk together flour, baking soda, salt, and granulated sugar until well blended. Add softened butter, sour cream, and vanilla; increase speed to medium-high and beat until smooth (2 minutes). Add chocolate-rum mixture and eggs and beat until well blended (1 minute). Pour batter over pecan topping, spreading evenly.

5.   Bake 50 to 55 minutes or until cake tester inserted in center comes out clean. Remove pan to wire rack. Cool 10 minutes before loosening cake from pan with a knife and inverting onto serving platter. Finish cooling on platter. Serve with ice cream, if desired.

Yield: One 12-cup bundt cake.

Old-Fashioned Devil's Food Cake

2 cups sifted cake flour
2 teaspoons baking soda
½ teaspoon salt
½ cup butter, softened
1 cup granulated sugar
1 cup firmly packed light brown
  sugar

3 eggs, lightly beaten
3 squares (3 ounces) unsweetened
  chocolate, melted and cooled
1 teaspoon vanilla extract
1¼ cups buttermilk
Chocolate–Sour Cream Frosting
  (page 141)

1. Position rack in center of oven; preheat to 350°F. Grease two 8-inch round pans; line with waxed paper; grease; dust with flour.

2. Sift together flour, baking soda, and salt; set aside.

3. In a large bowl, and using electric beaters, cream butter until light and smooth. Gradually add granulated and brown sugar, beating well after each addition. Pour in eggs, a little at a time, beating until mixture is light, smooth, and fluffy. Beat in melted chocolate and vanilla.

4. Using a large rubber spatula, alternately stir in dry ingredients and buttermilk, beginning and ending with dry ingredients, and blending well after each addition. Pour batter into prepared pans, dividing equally.

5. Bake 25 to 30 minutes, or until cake tester inserted in center comes out clean. Remove pans to wire racks, and cool for 10 minutes. Run the tip of a sharp knife between cake and pan to loosen. Invert pans onto other racks; gently peel off waxed paper. Place paper loosely on layers and invert onto other racks; finish cooling right side up on racks.

6. Wrap each layer in plastic and freeze until firm. Using a sharp serrated knife, cut each layer in half horizontally to make a total of four thin layers. Place one layer on inverted cake pan; spread with ¾ cup Sour Cream Frosting. Repeat with next two layers. Place last layer on top; frost top and sides with remaining frosting. (If you prefer a whipped cream frosting, beat 2¼ cups heavy cream with 5 tablespoons granulated sugar until soft peaks form. Add 1 teaspoon vanilla extract and beat until stiff. Fill and frost as above.)

Yield: One 8-inch round cake.

Rich Chocolate Cake

I admit it, this is not an old-fashioned cake. But it is so sinfully delicious, I just had to share it with you.

½ cup plus 2 tablespoons butter
16 squares (16 ounces) semisweet
   chocolate
4 eggs
2 tablespoons granulated sugar

1 tablespoon flour
1 cup Sweetened Whipped Cream
   (page 156)
Fresh strawberries or raspberries
   (optional)

1.   Position rack in center of oven; preheat to 400°F. Grease bottom of an 8-inch springform pan; line with waxed paper; grease paper. Do not dust with flour.

2.   Melt butter and chocolate in the top of a double boiler over simmering water; remove top pan from water and set aside.

3.   Put eggs and sugar in bowl of electric mixer; set over hot, not simmering, water, and whisk 1 to 2 minutes, until sugar dissolves and mixture darkens and becomes lukewarm. Remove from heat and beat with electric beaters 4 to 5 minutes, until mixture thickens and triples in volume. Sprinkle flour over eggs and gently fold it in with a rubber spatula.

4.   Fold one third of the egg mixture into chocolate mixture, then fold chocolate mixture into remaining egg mixture. Pour batter into prepared pan. Gently tap pan on work surface two or three times to remove any large air bubbles.

5.   Bake 15 minutes. Remove pan to wire rack. Cool completely. *Do not remove outer rim of pan.* Cover with several layers of plastic wrap and freeze at least 6 hours or up to 1 month.

6.   Before serving, remove cake from freezer and run a knife around edge; release rim. Invert cake onto serving platter and remove waxed paper. Spread whipped cream over cake. Top with fresh berries, if desired. Refrigerate until 15 minutes before serving. Serve small slices.

Yield: One 8-inch round cake.

Preacher's Chocolate Cake

2½ cups all-purpose flour
2 teaspoons baking soda
¼ teaspoon salt
1 cup butter, softened
1¾ cups granulated sugar
2 eggs, lightly beaten

2 teaspoons vanilla extract
2 squares (2 ounces) unsweetened
    chocolate, melted
1 cup sour cream
1 cup boiling water
Confectioners' sugar

1. Position rack in lower third of oven; preheat to 325°F. Grease a 10- by 4-inch tube pan or a 12-cup bundt pan; dust with flour.

2. In a medium bowl, whisk or stir together flour, baking soda, and salt; set aside.

3. In a large bowl, and using electric beaters, cream butter until light and smooth. Add sugar in several additions, beating until mixture is light and fluffy. Gradually add eggs, beating until mixture has the consistency of lightly whipped cream. Beat in vanilla and melted chocolate.

4. Using a large rubber spatula, alternately stir in dry ingredients and sour cream, beginning and ending with dry ingredients, and blending well after each addition. Add the boiling water all at once, stirring until well blended. Pour batter into prepared pan, spreading evenly.

5. Bake 50 to 55 minutes, or until cake tester inserted in center comes out clean. Remove pan to wire rack. Cool 15 minutes before loosening cake from pan with a knife and removing. Finish cooling right side up on rack. Dust with confectioners' sugar just before serving.

Yield: One 10- by 4-inch cake.

Mississippi Mud Cake

This cake is dark, delicious, and very rich. Serve skinny slices.

1¼ cups flour
½ teaspoon salt
¾ cup butter, softened
1½ cups granulated sugar
4 eggs, lightly beaten
1 teaspoon vanilla extract

8 squares (8 ounces) semisweet
chocolate, melted and cooled
1 cup (one 6-ounce package)
chocolate chips
1 cup chopped pecans
Unsweetened whipped cream

1.   Position rack in center of oven; preheat to 350°F. Grease a 9-inch spring-form pan; dust with flour.

2.   In a medium bowl, whisk or stir together flour and salt.

3.   In a large bowl, and using electric beaters, cream butter until light and smooth. Add sugar in several additions, beating until mixture is light and fluffy. Gradually add eggs, beating until mixture has the consistency of lightly whipped cream. Stir in vanilla and melted chocolate.

4.   Using a large rubber spatula, gradually stir dry ingredients into chocolate mixture until well blended; stir in chocolate chips and pecans. Pour batter into prepared pan, spreading evenly.

5.   Bake 35 to 40 minutes. The cake is done when the surface looks dry and cracked; underneath, the center will be soft and gooey. Remove pan to wire rack, and cool 10 minutes. Run a knife around sides of cake to loosen it from pan. Remove outer rim of pan; finish cooling on rack. Slide a long metal spatula under cake to loosen it from bottom of pan; transfer cake to a serving platter. Serve with unsweetened whipped cream.

Yield: One 9-inch round cake.

Texas Long Cake

This cake is especially easy to make and feeds a crowd.

3 squares (3 ounces) unsweetened
  chocolate
1 cup butter
1 cup water
2 cups all-purpose flour
2 cups granulated sugar
1 teaspoon baking powder

1 teaspoon baking soda
½ teaspoon salt
2 eggs
1 cup sour cream
1 teaspoon vanilla extract
Fast Fudge Frosting (page 148)

1.   Position rack in center of oven; preheat to 350°F. Grease an 11- by 18- by 1-inch sheet pan; dust with flour.

2.   In a medium saucepan, heat chocolate, butter, and the water until boiling. Lower heat and simmer just until butter melts; remove from heat.

3.   In a large bowl, and using electric beaters set on low speed, whisk together flour, sugar, baking powder, baking soda, and salt; pour hot chocolate mixture over dry ingredients and beat until blended. Increase speed to medium-high; add eggs, one at a time, beating 1 minute after each addition (mixture will be thin). Stir in sour cream and vanilla. Pour batter into prepared pan, spreading evenly.

4.   Bake 20 to 25 minutes, or until cake tester inserted in center comes out clean. Remove to wire rack; cool completely in pan. Frost with Fast Fudge Frosting.

Yield: One 11- by 18- by 1-inch cake.

CAKE CUE

The easiest and oldest cake decoration: Place a paper doily on top of an unfrosted chocolate or other dark-colored cake. Gently tap confectioners' sugar through a small-meshed strainer, over doily. Carefully remove doily to reveal design. (Use cocoa on a light-colored cake.)

63

Wellesley Fudge Cake

This cake dates back to the late 1800s, when two Wellesley College graduates wowed the customers in the Wellesley Tea Room with this confection.

*4 squares (4 ounces) unsweetened
    chocolate*
½ cup hot water
1½ cups granulated sugar
2 cups sifted cake flour
1 teaspoon baking soda

1 teaspoon salt
½ cup butter, softened
3 eggs, lightly beaten
1 teaspoon vanilla extract
⅔ cup milk
Classic Fudge Frosting (page 150)

1.   Position rack in center of oven; preheat to 350°F. Grease two 9-inch square pans; dust with flour.

2.   In the top of a double boiler over hot, not boiling, water, combine chocolate and the ½ cup water, stirring often until chocolate melts and mixture is smooth. Add ½ cup of the sugar, stirring about 2 minutes or until sugar dissolves. Remove top part of boiler from water; cool chocolate until warm to the touch.

3.   In a medium bowl, sift together flour, baking soda, and salt; set aside.

4.   In a large bowl, and using electric beaters, cream butter until light and smooth. Add remaining 1 cup sugar in several additions, beating until mixture is light and fluffy. Gradually add eggs, beating until mixture has the consistency of lightly whipped cream. Stir in vanilla and cooled chocolate.

5.   Using a large rubber spatula, alternately stir in dry ingredients and milk, beginning and ending with dry ingredients, and blending well after each addition. Pour batter into prepared pans, dividing equally.

6.   Bake 25 minutes, or until cake tester inserted in center comes out clean. Remove pans to wire racks. Cool 10 minutes before loosening cakes from pans with a knife and removing. Finish cooling right side up on racks.

7.   Spread frosting between layers and over top and sides of cake.

Yield: One 9-inch square cake.

Mexican Cake Roll

The combination of cinnamon and chocolate gives this cake its heady flavor.

5 squares (5 ounces) semisweet
   chocolate
2 teaspoons instant-coffee powder
¼ cup boiling water
5 egg yolks
¼ teaspoon ground cinnamon
½ cup sugar

⅛ teaspoon almond extract
5 egg whites
½ teaspoon cream of tartar
Unsweetened cocoa powder
Sweetened Whipped Cream (page
   156)

1.   Position rack in center of oven; preheat to 350°F. Grease an 11- by 17- by 1-inch jelly-roll pan; line with waxed paper; grease paper; dust with flour.

2.   In the top of a double boiler over simmering water, combine chocolate, coffee powder, and the boiling water, stirring often until chocolate melts and mixture is smooth. Remove top part of boiler from water; cool chocolate until warm to the touch.

3.   In a medium bowl, and using electric beaters, beat egg yolks on high speed until light and fluffy (about 3 minutes). Combine cinnamon and sugar; beat into yolks, 1 tablespoon at a time, beating well after each addition. Continue to beat until sugar is dissolved and mixture is very thick (about 5 minutes). Blend in melted chocolate and almond extract.

4.   In a separate bowl, beat egg whites until frothy; add cream of tartar and beat until whites stand in firm, moist, shiny peaks. Gently fold chocolate mixture into whites. Pour batter into prepared pan, spreading evenly.

5.   Bake 18 to 20 minutes, or until cake tester inserted in center comes out clean. Remove pan to wire rack and immediately cover cake with a slightly dampened tea towel until completely cool (about 30 minutes), then remove towel.

6.   *To assemble cake:* Use a small sharp knife to loosen edges of cake; then lightly dust cake with unsweetened cocoa powder. Place tea towel over cake, folding short ends under pan to secure the cake. Invert pan onto work surface. Remove pan and gently peel off waxed paper; trim any crusty edges. Spread Sweetened Whipped Cream to edge of cake. Using the towel as an aide, lift one long side and roll up the cake like a jelly roll. Sift cocoa powder over cake roll. Slide two long, wide spatulas under roll and carefully transfer to a serving platter. Cover with plastic wrap and chill thoroughly before serving.

Yield: 8 to 10 servings.

Cola Cake

Not for cola lovers only.

1½ cups all-purpose flour
1½ cups granulated sugar
½ teaspoon baking soda
¼ teaspoon salt
½ cup chopped pecans
¾ cup cola
2 tablespoons unsweetened cocoa
    powder

½ cup butter, cut into 8 pieces
1 egg, lightly beaten
½ cup buttermilk
1 teaspoon vanilla extract
Cola Icing (recipe follows)
¾ cup toasted, shredded coconut

CAKE CUE

*Eggs that are not
fresh will spoil the
taste and texture of
a cake. To test, place
egg in bowl with
enough cold water
to cover. If it sinks,
it's fresh.*

1.   Position rack in center of oven; preheat to 350°F. Grease a 9-inch square baking pan; line bottom with aluminum foil, allowing ends of foil to extend about 2 inches over sides of pan; grease foil and dust with flour.

2.   In a large bowl, whisk or stir together flour, sugar, baking soda, and salt. On a sheet of waxed paper, mix pecans with 2 teaspoons of the dry ingredients; set aside.

3.   In a small, heavy saucepan over medium heat, combine cola, cocoa powder, and butter, stirring constantly until butter is melted. Pour hot cola mixture over dry ingredients; add egg, buttermilk, and vanilla, beating until mixture is dark and well blended. Stir in pecans. Pour batter into prepared pan, spreading evenly.

4.   Bake 30 to 35 minutes, or until cake tester inserted in center comes out clean. While cake is baking, prepare Cola Icing.

5.   When cake is done, remove pan to wire rack. Pour Cola Icing over hot cake, tilting pan to spread evenly. Sprinkle toasted coconut over icing. Cool cake in pan 15 minutes. Using foil ends as handles, lift cake and place on wire rack to finish cooling.

Yield: One 9-inch square cake.

Cola Icing

2 tablespoons butter
3 tablespoons cola
1 tablespoon unsweetened cocoa
   powder

1½ cups confectioners' sugar
½ teaspoon vanilla extract

In a medium-sized, heavy saucepan, combine butter, cola, and cocoa powder; stir over low heat until butter is melted. Remove from heat; stir in confectioners' sugar and vanilla until well combined.

Yield: About ½ cup.

Angel Food, Sponge, and Chiffon Cakes

Angel food, sponge, and chiffon cakes are also known as foam cakes. These cakes rely heavily on air and steam for leavening. To achieve the best volume, you should always use eggs that have been warmed to room temperature before beating them.

The batter for angel food, chiffon, and *some* sponge cakes is baked in *ungreased pans*, allowing it to climb the sides of the pan. (Grease would make them slide down and collapse on themselves.) These cakes are light, airy, and delicious, and make a wonderful base for almost any combination of fillings and frostings.

Sunshine Sponge Cake

This cake was probably created to avoid wasting the yolks left over from making angel food cake.

1¾ cups sifted cake flour
½ teaspoon salt
2¼ teaspoons baking powder
12 egg yolks

1¼ cups granulated sugar
1 cup freshly squeezed orange
   juice or water
1 teaspoon vanilla extract

   1.   Position rack in lower third of oven; preheat to 325°F. Have ready an ungreased 10- by 4-inch tube pan.

   2.   Sift together cake flour, salt, and baking powder; set aside.

   3.   In a large bowl, and using electric beaters set on high speed, beat egg yolks until thick and lemon-colored (5 to 10 minutes). Add sugar, a few table-spoons at a time, beating well after each addition. Stir in orange juice and vanilla.

   4.   Gradually sift dry ingredients over yolks and, using a large rubber spatula, fold in gently but thoroughly after each addition. Spoon batter into ungreased pan, spreading evenly.

   5.   Bake 1 hour, or until cake tester inserted in center comes out clean. Remove pan from oven and immediately invert onto a funnel to cool completely. When cake is completely cooled, run a long, slim knife between cake and pan to loosen and remove cake.

Yield: One 10- by 4-inch tube cake.

Angel Food Cake with Mocha Cream Filling

For a cholesterol-free treat, serve unfilled Angel Food Cake with Raspberry-Peach Sauce (page 152).

Mocha Cream Filling (recipe follows)
1 cup sifted cake flour
¾ cup confectioners' sugar
12 egg whites
¼ teaspoon salt

1½ teaspoons cream of tartar
¾ cup granulated sugar
1 teaspoon vanilla extract
½ teaspoon almond extract
1 cup cold heavy cream

1.   Make Mocha Cream Filling.
2.   Position rack in lower third of oven; preheat to 375°F. Have ready an ungreased 10- by 4-inch angel food tube pan with removable bottom.
3.   Sift together flour and confectioners' sugar; set aside.
4.   In a large bowl, and using electric beaters, beat egg whites and salt until foamy; add cream of tartar, beating until whites form soft peaks. Add granulated sugar, a few tablespoons at a time, beating until whites stand in stiff, moist, shiny peaks. Stir in vanilla and almond extracts.
5.   Gradually sift dry ingredients over whites. Using a large rubber spatula, fold them in gently but thoroughly after each addition. Pour batter into un-greased pan. Gently tap pan on work surface two or three times to remove any large air bubbles.
6.   Bake 45 minutes, or until cake tester inserted in center comes out clean. Remove pan from oven and immediately invert onto a funnel to cool completely (about 2 hours). When cool, loosen sides of cake with a long metal spatula and lift out center of pan with cake on it. Carefully loosen bottom and central core of cake with a thin, sharp knife.

Wrap cake in plastic and freeze until firm. Using a sharp serrated knife, cut cake horizontally to make four even layers. Place bottom layer right side up on serving platter. Spread one third of the Mocha Cream Filling over top. Repeat with next two layers. Place top layer over cream filling. Wrap lightly in plastic and refrigerate at least 1 hour.

7.   In a deep metal or glass bowl, and using electric beaters, beat cream until thick; cover and refrigerate. Just before serving cake, spread whipped cream around sides and over top of cake.

Yield: One 10- by 4-inch angel food cake.

Mocha Cream Filling

3 cups milk
½ cup cornstarch
1⅓ cups granulated sugar
½ cup unsweetened cocoa powder
2 tablespoons instant-coffee
  powder

¼ teaspoon salt
3 egg yolks, lightly beaten
3 tablespoons butter, cut into
  small pieces
2 teaspoons vanilla extract

1.   In a small, heavy saucepan, warm milk over medium heat until tiny bubbles appear around edge of pan; set aside.

2.   In the top of a double boiler, combine cornstarch, sugar, cocoa powder, powdered coffee, and salt; gradually add milk, stirring constantly. Cook and stir over simmering water until thick (about 15 minutes).

3.   Gradually spoon 4 or 5 tablespoons hot milk mixture into yolks, stirring until yolks are warmed. Slowly pour yolks into remaining milk mixture; cook 5 minutes, stirring frequently. Transfer mixture to a bowl; add butter and vanilla, stirring until butter melts. Cool to room temperature; cover with plastic wrap and refrigerate until chilled.

Yield: About 3 cups.

Orange-Walnut Passover Sponge Cake

¾ cup cake meal
1 cup finely chopped walnuts
½ teaspoon ground cinnamon
8 egg yolks
1¼ cups granulated sugar
1 cup freshly squeezed orange
  juice

1 tablespoon grated orange peel
8 egg whites
½ teaspoon salt
½ cup raspberry preserves
Confectioners' sugar

1. Position rack in center of oven; preheat to 350°F. Grease two 8-inch round cake pans; line with waxed paper; grease; dust with flour.

2. In a medium bowl, whisk or stir together cake meal, chopped walnuts, and cinnamon; set aside.

3. In a large bowl, and using electric beaters, beat yolks until blended. Gradually add 1 cup of the sugar, beating until yolks are thick, almost white, and tripled in volume. Gradually beat in orange juice; stir in orange peel.

4. In a separate bowl, and using clean beaters, beat whites and salt until frothy; gradually add remaining ¼ cup sugar, beating until whites stand in stiff, moist, shiny peaks.

5. Fold yolk mixture into beaten egg whites. Gradually add cake meal mixture, folding carefully but completely after each addition. Pour batter into prepared pans, dividing evenly.

6. Bake 35 to 40 minutes, or until cake tester inserted in center of cake comes out clean. Remove pans to wire racks, and cool for 10 minutes. Run the tip of a sharp knife between cake and pan to loosen. Invert pans onto other racks; gently peel off waxed paper. Place paper loosely on layers and invert onto other racks; finish cooling on racks.

7. Place one layer right side up on serving platter; spread with raspberry preserves. Place next layer wrong side up; dust top with confectioners' sugar.

Yield: One 8-inch round cake.

Lemon Génoise

6 eggs
1 cup granulated sugar
1 teaspoon vanilla extract
2 teaspoons grated lemon peel
1 cup sifted all-purpose flour

½ cup butter, clarified and cooled
   (see Note)
Lemon Buttercream Frosting
   (page 142)

1.   Position rack in center of oven; preheat to 350°F. Grease two 9-inch round cake pans; line with waxed paper; grease; dust with flour.

2.   In a large bowl, combine eggs and sugar. Set bowl over hot, not simmering, water, and stir with a wire whisk until sugar dissolves and mixture is lukewarm. Remove bowl. Set electric mixer on highest speed, and beat eggs and sugar until cool, light, thick, and quadrupled in volume. (Mixture should be as thick as mayonnaise.) Beat in vanilla and lemon peel.

3.   Sift ¼ cup of the flour into egg mixture; fold in gently but thoroughly. Repeat procedure until all the flour has been incorporated.

4.   Whisk ½ cup batter into clarified butter until well blended. Add this mixture, ¼ cup at a time, to remaining batter; fold gently but thoroughly after each addition. Pour batter into prepared pans, dividing equally. Tilt each pan so that a thin coat of batter clings to the inside wall. Gently tap pans on work surface two or three times to remove any large air bubbles.

5.   Bake 25 to 30 minutes, or until cake tester inserted in center comes out clean. Remove pans to wire racks, and immediately run the tip of a sharp knife between cake and pan to loosen. Invert pans onto other racks; gently peel off waxed paper. Place paper loosely on layers and invert onto other racks; finish cooling on racks. Fill and frost with Lemon Buttercream Frosting.

Yield: One 9-inch layer cake.

Note: To clarify butter, melt butter over very low heat in a small saucepan. Transfer butter to a measuring cup and let cool 30 minutes, without stirring. When cool, use a teaspoon to skim off any tiny specks of white milk solids that remain floating on top (most of them will have settled to bottom of cup). Pour clear butter into a small bowl, and discard milky residue left on bottom of cup.

   Chocolate Génoise: Substitute ½ cup unsweetened cocoa powder for ½ cup flour. Omit lemon peel and substitute 2 teaspoons grated orange peel. Fill and frost with Chocolate Buttercream Frosting (page 142), using 1 tablespoon orange-flavored liqueur in place of 1 tablespoon milk.

Not-So-Lazy Daisy Cake

Lazy Daisy Cake was first conceived in the 1930s when oven broilers were introduced to homemakers. The topping was broiled on the cake instead of baked, making it a "lazy" method of baking. Either way, this cake is good.

Cake

1½ cups flour
1½ teaspoons baking powder
½ teaspoon salt
3 eggs, lightly beaten

1¼ cups granulated sugar
1½ teaspoons vanilla extract
¾ cup milk
2 tablespoons butter

Topping

¼ cup melted butter
¼ cup firmly packed light brown
  sugar

¼ cup milk
½ cup flaked coconut
¼ cup chopped walnuts

1. Position rack in center of oven; preheat to 350°F. Grease a 9-inch square baking pan; dust with flour.
2. *To make cake:* In a small bowl, whisk or stir together flour, baking powder, and salt.
3. In a large bowl, and using electric beaters, beat eggs, granulated sugar, and vanilla until thick and lemon-colored. Using a large rubber spatula, gradually stir in dry ingredients, blending well after each addition.
4. In a small saucepan over low heat, combine milk and butter. Stir constantly until very hot, then pour into batter all at once; stir until well blended. Pour batter into prepared pan.
5. Bake 30 minutes, or until cake tester inserted in center comes out clean.
6. *To make topping:* While cake is baking, combine topping ingredients until well blended. Spread evenly over hot cake and bake 5 minutes, or until lightly browned. Cool cake in pan on rack. Loosen edges with a sharp knife and invert onto rack; invert right side up on serving platter.

Yield: One 9-inch square cake.

Old-Fashioned Jam Roll

5 eggs, at room temperature
¾ cup granulated sugar
1½ teaspoons vanilla extract
1 teaspoon grated lemon peel
1 cup sifted cake flour

½ teaspoon baking powder
¼ teaspoon salt
¾ cup good-quality, thick jam
Confectioners' sugar

1. Position rack in center of oven; preheat to 400°F. Grease a 10½- by 15½- by 1-inch jelly-roll pan; line bottom and sides with waxed paper; grease entire surface of paper; dust with flour.

2. In a large bowl, beat eggs until frothy. Add sugar, 1 tablespoon at a time, and beat until eggs thicken and triple in volume (about 10 minutes). Beat in vanilla and lemon peel.

3. Sift together flour, baking powder, and salt. Add ¼ cup at a time to egg mixture, folding in gently but thoroughly after each addition. Pour batter into prepared pan, pushing it into corners and smoothing top with a spatula.

4. Bake 10 to 12 minutes, or until surface of cake is golden brown and a cake tester inserted in center comes out clean.

5. While cake is baking, dampen a clean dish towel. When cake is done, remove pan to a wire rack and immediately loosen edges of cake with the tip of a sharp knife. Cover cake with the dampened towel and place in the refrigerator 15 minutes, or until cool.

6. Pull ends of towel tautly to secure cake, and invert pan onto work surface. Lift pan and gently peel off waxed paper; trim off any crusty edges with a long serrated knife. Spread jam evenly over cake.

7. Starting from short end, roll up cake using towel to help roll and lift cake. Place cake on a serving platter, seam side down, and dust with confectioners' sugar.

Yield: 8 to 10 servings.

CAKE CUE

Instead of making a traditional jelly-roll cake, cool the cake unrolled on a wire rack, then slice lengthwise in half or thirds. Spread layers with jam, frosting, or your favorite filling; stack and dust with confectioners' sugar.

Marmalade-Glazed Orange Cake

1½ cups all-purpose flour
½ teaspoon salt
6 egg yolks
1½ cups granulated sugar
½ cup freshly squeezed orange
  juice
1 tablespoon grated orange peel

6 egg whites
¼ teaspoon cream of tartar
Orange Marmalade Glaze (recipe
  follows)
¼ cup slivered blanched almonds,
  toasted

1. Position rack in lower third of oven; preheat to 350°F. Have ready an ungreased 10- by 4-inch tube pan. (Don't use one with a removable bottom.)

2. In a small bowl, whisk or stir together flour and salt; set aside.

3. In a large bowl, and using electric beaters, beat egg yolks on high speed until thick and lemon-colored (5 to 10 minutes). Add 1 cup of the sugar in several additions, beating until mixture is smooth (about 3 minutes).

4. Using a large rubber spatula, alternately stir in dry ingredients and orange juice, beginning and ending with dry ingredients, and blending well after each addition. Stir in orange peel.

5. In a separate bowl, and using clean beaters, beat whites until frothy; add cream of tartar and beat until soft peaks form. Gradually add remaining ½ cup sugar, beating until whites stand in stiff, moist, shiny peaks. Fold one third of the whites into batter; fold in remaining whites. Pour batter into ungreased pan, spreading evenly.

6. Bake 50 to 55 minutes, or until cake tester inserted in center comes out clean. Remove pan to wire rack. Cool 10 minutes before loosening cake from pan with a knife and removing. Finish cooling right side up on rack. Prepare Orange Marmalade Glaze.

7. Pierce top and sides of cake in several places with a toothpick. Brush on glaze; sprinkle almonds over top.

Yield: One 10- by 4-inch tube cake.

Orange Marmalade Glaze

³/₄ cup orange juice
¹/₄ cup orange liqueur
¹/₄ cup orange marmalade

In a small, heavy saucepan, gently heat orange juice, orange liqueur, and marmalade, stirring constantly until marmalade is dissolved.

Yield: About 1 cup.

Orange Chiffon Cake

This classic was introduced in 1948 to promote the use of oil in cakes. It's delicious either plain, frosted, with fruit, or any other way your heart desires.

2 cups all-purpose flour
3 teaspoons baking powder
1 teaspoon salt
1½ cups granulated sugar
½ cup vegetable oil
6 egg yolks
¾ cup freshly squeezed orange
  juice

1 tablespoon grated orange peel
2 teaspoons vanilla extract
6 egg whites
½ teaspoon cream of tartar
Grand Marnier Filling and
  Frosting (page 144) or
  confectioners' sugar (optional)

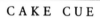

CAKE CUE

Overbeaten egg whites can be salvaged by briefly beating an egg white into the overbeaten whites. Use 1 white for every 3 or 4 overbeaten whites.

1.   Position rack in lower third of oven; preheat to 325°F. Have ready an ungreased 10- by 4-inch tube pan with a removable bottom.

2.   In a large bowl, whisk together flour, baking powder, sugar, and salt. Make a well in center of dry ingredients; add oil, egg yolks, orange juice, orange peel, and vanilla, and beat until batter is smooth and well blended.

3.   In a separate bowl, and using electric beaters, beat whites until frothy; add cream of tartar and beat until whites stand in stiff, moist, shiny peaks. Gradually pour batter over whites, folding only until blended. Pour batter into ungreased tube pan, spreading evenly.

4.   Bake 1 hour and 10 minutes, or until cake tester inserted in center comes out clean. Invert pan onto a funnel and let cake cool completely in pan (about 2 hours). When cool, loosen sides of cake with a long metal spatula and lift out center of pan with cake on it. Carefully loosen bottom and central core of cake with a thin, sharp knife. Invert right side up onto a serving plate. If desired, fill and frost with Grand Marnier Filling and Frosting, or sprinkle with confectioners' sugar.

Yield: One 10- by 4-inch tube cake.

Chocolate Chip Chiffon Cake: Omit orange juice and peel; substitute ¾ cup cold water and 1 cup miniature chocolate chips.

Marble Chiffon Cake

3 squares (3 ounces) unsweetened
   chocolate, coarsely chopped
3 tablespoons granulated sugar
¼ cup boiling water
2 cups all-purpose flour
1½ cups granulated sugar
3 teaspoons baking powder
1 teaspoon salt

½ cup vegetable oil
7 egg yolks
¾ cup cold water
2 teaspoons vanilla extract
2 tablespoons grated orange peel
7 egg whites
½ teaspoon cream of tartar

1. Position rack in lower third of oven; preheat to 325°F. Have ready an ungreased 10- by 4-inch tube pan with removable bottom.

2. In a medium bowl, combine chocolate, the 3 tablespoons sugar, and the boiling water, stirring until chocolate melts and sugar dissolves. Set aside to cool.

3. In a large bowl, whisk or stir together flour, the 1½ cups sugar, baking powder, and salt. Make a well in center and add oil, egg yolks, the cold water, vanilla, and orange peel. Beat until smooth and well blended.

4. In a separate bowl, and using electric beaters, beat egg whites until frothy; add cream of tartar and beat until whites stand in stiff, moist, shiny peaks. Gradually pour egg yolk mixture over whites, folding only until blended. Fold one third of the batter into cooled chocolate.

5. Fill ungreased pan, alternating large spoonfuls of light batter with small spoonfuls of chocolate batter. Draw a narrow spatula or knife through the batter to form the marbling.

6. Bake 55 minutes, or until cake tester inserted in center comes out clean. Remove from oven and immediately invert pan onto a funnel. Cool cake completely in pan (about 2 hours). When cool, loosen sides of cake with a long metal spatula and lift out center of pan with cake on it. Carefully loosen bottom and central core of cake with a thin, sharp knife. Invert right side up onto a serving plate.

Yield: One 10- by 4-inch tube cake.

Coconut Chiffon Cake with Pineapple-Rum Topping

2 cups all-purpose flour
1¾ cups granulated sugar
3 teaspoons baking powder
½ teaspoon salt
½ cup vegetable oil
6 egg yolks
¾ cup cold water

1 cup flaked coconut
2 teaspoons vanilla extract
6 egg whites
¼ teaspoon cream of tartar
Pineapple-Rum Topping (recipe
    follows)

1. Position rack in lower third of oven; preheat to 325°F. Have ready an ungreased 10- by 4-inch tube pan with removable bottom.

2. In a large bowl, whisk together flour, 1½ cups of the sugar, baking powder, and salt. Make a well in the center; add oil, egg yolks, the water, coconut, and vanilla. Beat until smooth.

3. In another large bowl, and using electric beaters, beat egg whites until frothy; add cream of tartar and continue beating until soft peaks form. Add remaining ¼ cup sugar, a few tablespoons at a time, beating until whites stand in stiff, moist, shiny peaks. Gradually pour batter over whites, folding only until blended. Pour batter into ungreased tube pan.

4. Bake 1 hour and 10 minutes, or until cake tester inserted in center comes out clean. Invert pan onto a funnel and let cake cool completely in pan (about 2 hours). When cool, loosen sides of cake with a long metal spatula and lift out center of pan with cake on it. Carefully loosen bottom and central core of cake with a thin, sharp knife. Invert right side up onto another wire rack; place rack onto a sheet of waxed paper (to catch drippings from glaze), and pierce cake all over with a toothpick.

5. Prepare Pineapple-Rum Topping. Spoon warm topping over cake. Cool completely before serving.

Yield: One 10- by 4-inch tube cake.

Pineapple-Rum Topping

¾ *cup pineapple preserves*
¼ *cup freshly squeezed lemon*
  juice

1½ *cups confectioners' sugar*
¼ *cup light rum*

1. Spoon pineapple preserves evenly over cake.
2. In a small, heavy saucepan over low heat, combine lemon juice and confectioners' sugar, stirring until just smooth. Remove from heat and stir in rum.

Yield: About 1 cup.

Loaf Cakes and Cakes with Fruit and Nuts

Banana-Walnut Loaf Cake

2⅔ cups all-purpose flour
2 teaspoons baking soda
¾ teaspoon salt
1½ teaspoons ground cinnamon
1½ cups chopped walnuts

4 eggs, lightly beaten
1⅔ cups granulated sugar
1 cup safflower oil
½ cup sour cream
2 cups mashed ripe banana

1. Position rack in center of oven; preheat to 350°F. Grease two 9- by 5- by 2¾-inch loaf pans; dust with flour.

2. In a medium bowl, whisk or stir together flour, baking soda, salt, and cinnamon. Toss walnuts with 2 teaspoons dry ingredients; set aside.

3. In a large bowl, and using electric beaters set on low, beat eggs until frothy. Add sugar in several additions and beat until well blended. Gradually pour in oil, beating until well emulsified. Stir in sour cream and mashed bananas.

4. Using a large rubber spatula, gradually stir in dry ingredients, blending well after each addition. Stir in walnuts. Pour batter in prepared pans, dividing equally.

5. Bake 50 to 60 minutes, or until cake tester inserted in center of cakes comes out clean. Remove pans to wire racks. Cool 10 minutes before loosening cakes from pans with a knife and removing. Finish cooling right side up on racks. Wrap loaves in plastic for 24 hours to allow flavors to develop.

Yield: Two 9- by 5- by 2¾-inch loaves.

White Fruit Cake

Cake

3/4 cup diced candied apricot
1 1/4 cups diced candied pineapple
1/2 cup diced candied kiwifruit
1/2 cup diced candied orange peel
1/2 cup diced candied lemon peel
1/2 cup diced candied citron
1/2 cup halved candied cherries
1 cup golden raisins
3/4 cup blanched, toasted, slivered
    almonds
1 1/3 cups flaked coconut
2 cups all-purpose flour

1 1/2 teaspoons baking powder
1/2 teaspoon ground allspice
1/4 teaspoon ground mace
1/4 teaspoon ground cloves
1/2 teaspoon salt
1 cup butter, softened
1 cup granulated sugar
5 eggs, lightly beaten
1 teaspoon vanilla extract
1/2 cup brandy, rum, or bourbon,
    plus brandy for soaking cake

Glaze

1/4 cup light corn syrup
3 tablespoons water
Nuts and candied fruit, for
    garnish

1. Position rack in center of oven; preheat to 300°F. Position another rack on the lowest shelf; fill a large, shallow pan with water, and place on lower rack. Grease two 8 1/2- by 4 1/2- by 2 1/2-inch loaf pans; line with heavy brown paper or parchment paper; grease.

2. *To make cake:* In a large bowl, combine fruit, peels, citron, cherries, raisins, almonds, and coconut. In a medium bowl, whisk or stir together flour, baking powder, allspice, mace, cloves, and salt. Mix 1/4 cup dry ingredients with fruits; set aside.

3. In a large bowl, and using electric beaters, cream butter until light and smooth. Add sugar in several additions, beating until mixture is light and fluffy. Gradually add eggs, beating until mixture has the consistency of lightly whipped cream. Beat in vanilla.

4. Using a large rubber spatula, alternately stir in dry ingredients and brandy, beginning and ending with dry ingredients, and blending well after each addition. Add fruit and nut mixture, stirring until fruits are evenly distributed throughout batter. Pour batter into prepared pans, dividing evenly.

5. Bake 2 hours, or until cake tester inserted in center comes out clean. Remove pans to wire racks. Cool 20 minutes before loosening cakes from pans with a knife and removing. Carefully peel off paper; finish cooling right side up on rack.

6. Cut two pieces of cheesecloth large enough to hold each cake; soak in brandy or other liquor. Wrap cooled cakes in cheesecloth, then wrap snugly in one layer of plastic and one layer of aluminum foil. Store in a cool spot, or refrigerate at least three weeks before slicing.

7. *To make glaze:* Before serving, combine light corn syrup and the water in a small saucepan. Bring to a boil; cool to lukewarm. Brush on cold cake; garnish cake with nuts and bits of fruit, and brush again with warm glaze.

Yield: Two 8½- by 4½- by 2½-inch loaves.

Carrot Cake with Cream Cheese Frosting

1½ cups all-purpose flour
1 cup whole wheat flour
2 teaspoons baking soda
2 teaspoons baking powder
1½ teaspoons ground cinnamon
¼ teaspoon salt
3 eggs, lightly beaten
1½ cups firmly packed light
  brown sugar
1¼ cups vegetable oil

2 teaspoons vanilla extract
¾ cup (one 8-ounce can) drained,
  crushed pineapple
3 cups (5 to 6 large) grated raw
  carrots
1 cup chopped pecans
1 cup miniature chocolate chips
3½ cups flaked coconut
Cream Cheese Frosting (page
  157)

1.   Position rack in center of oven; preheat to 350°F. Grease a 9- by 13- by 2-inch cake pan; dust with flour.

2.   In a medium bowl, whisk or stir together flours, baking soda, baking powder, cinnamon, and salt; set aside.

3.   In a large bowl, and using electric beaters, beat eggs until frothy; add sugar in several additions and beat until well blended. Gradually pour in oil, beating until well emulsified. Beat in vanilla.

4.   Using a large rubber spatula, gradually stir in dry ingredients. Fold in pineapple, carrots, pecans, chocolate chips, and 1 cup of the coconut. Pour batter into prepared pan, spreading evenly.

5.   Bake 30 to 40 minutes, or until cake tester inserted in center comes out clean. Remove pan to wire rack. Cool completely before loosening cake from pan with a knife and removing. Frost top and sides with Cream Cheese Frosting. Sprinkle remaining 2½ cups coconut over top and sides of cake.

Yield: 9- by 13- by 2-inch cake.

Tennessee Jam Cake

2⅓ cups all-purpose flour
½ cup unsweetened cocoa powder
1 teaspoon baking soda
1 teaspoon ground cinnamon
¼ teaspoon ground ginger
¼ teaspoon ground nutmeg
¼ teaspoon ground cloves
1 cup chopped pecans
1 cup raisins
⅔ cup buttermilk

3 tablespoons whiskey, bourbon,
  or fruit juice
1 teaspoon vanilla extract
1 cup butter, softened
1 cup firmly packed dark brown
  sugar
1 cup granulated sugar
3 eggs, lightly beaten
1 cup thick blackberry jam
Confectioners' sugar

1. Position rack in lower third of oven; preheat to 350°F. Grease a 12-cup bundt pan or a 10- by 4-inch tube; dust with flour.

2. In a medium bowl, whisk or stir together flour, cocoa powder, baking soda, cinnamon, ginger, nutmeg, and cloves. On a sheet of waxed paper, mix pecans and raisins with 1 tablespoon dry ingredients; set aside.

3. Combine buttermilk, whiskey, and vanilla in a measuring cup; set aside.

4. In a large bowl, and using electric beaters, cream butter until light and smooth. Add sugars in several additions, beating until mixture is light and fluffy. Gradually add eggs, beating until mixture has the consistency of lightly whipped cream. Stir in blackberry jam.

5. Using a large rubber spatula, alternately stir in dry ingredients and buttermilk mixture, beginning and ending with dry ingredients, and blending well after each addition. Stir in pecans and raisins. Pour batter into prepared pan, spreading evenly.

6. Bake 55 to 60 minutes, or until cake tester inserted in center of cake comes out clean.

7. Remove pan to wire rack. Cool 15 minutes before loosening cake from pan with a knife and removing. Finish cooling right side up on rack. Wrap cake in plastic wrap and store in refrigerator at least 48 hours to mellow flavors. Serve at room temperature. Dust top with confectioners' sugar just before serving.

Yield: One 12-cup bundt cake.

Pennsylvania Dutch Apple Cake

3 cups peeled, cored, and thinly
   sliced tart apples
²/₃ cup granulated sugar mixed
   with 1 teaspoon ground
   cinnamon
¼ cup butter
2 tablespoons freshly squeezed
   lemon juice
1 teaspoon grated lemon peel

1⅓ cups cake flour
1½ teaspoons baking powder
¾ cup granulated sugar
½ teaspoon salt
¼ cup butter, softened
½ cup milk
2 egg yolks
1 teaspoon vanilla extract
Ice cream (optional)

1.   Position rack in center of oven; preheat to 375°F. Lightly grease a deep 9-inch pie plate.

2.   Arrange sliced apples in a circle so that bottom of plate is entirely covered; sprinkle cinnamon sugar on top.

3.   In a small saucepan, melt butter; add lemon juice and peel, and pour evenly over apples.

4.   In a medium bowl, whisk or stir together flour, baking powder, sugar, and salt. Add butter, milk, egg yolks, and vanilla, and beat on low speed until smooth and well blended. Pour batter over apple mixture, spreading evenly.

5.   Bake 30 to 35 minutes, or until cake tester inserted in center comes out clean. Remove pan to wire rack. Cool 15 minutes. Serve warm with ice cream, if desired.

Yield: One 9-inch round cake.

Down Cake

¾ cup granulated sugar
2 teaspoons baking powder
¼ teaspoon salt
⅔ cup milk
1 teaspoon vanilla extract
1 egg, lightly beaten

to 350°F. Melt 4 tablespoons of
e pan; spread over bottom and
neapple slice in center of pan;
center slice. Insert 1 maraschino
eapple.
gether flour, sugar, baking pow-
butter into pea-sized pieces; add
egg, and beat until smooth. Pour

ster inserted in center comes out
before loosening cake from pan
erve hot or warm.

Yield: One 9-inch round cake.

93

Dutch Apple Cake with Caramel Glaze

This apple cake is outstanding by itself and is an extra-special treat when served with vanilla ice cream.

2 cups all-purpose flour
1 teaspoon baking soda
1 teaspoon salt
1½ teaspoons ground cinnamon
3 eggs
1¾ cups granulated sugar
¾ cup vegetable oil

1 teaspoon vanilla extract
1 tablespoon freshly squeezed
  lemon juice
1 cup chopped walnuts
4 cups (4 or 5 medium) peeled,
  cored, and diced tart apples
Caramel Glaze (recipe follows)

1. Position rack in lower third of oven; preheat to 350°F. Grease a 12-cup bundt pan or a 10- by 4-inch tube pan; dust with flour.

2. In a medium bowl, whisk or stir together flour, baking soda, salt, and cinnamon; set aside.

3. In a large bowl, and using electric beaters set on low speed, beat eggs until frothy; add sugar in several additions and beat until well blended. Gradually pour in oil, beating until well emulsified. Beat in vanilla and lemon juice.

4. Using a large rubber spatula, gradually stir in dry ingredients. Fold in walnuts and apples. Pour batter into prepared pan, spreading evenly.

5. Bake 50 to 60 minutes, or until cake tester inserted in center comes out clean. Remove pan to wire rack. Cool 10 minutes before inverting onto another rack to cool completely. Prepare Caramel Glaze. Brush glaze over top and sides of warm cake. Serve cake warm or cold.

Yield: One 12-cup bundt cake.

Caramel Glaze

¼ *cup firmly packed dark brown*
  sugar
¼ *cup heavy cream*

2 *tablespoons butter*
2 *teaspoons light corn syrup*

Combine all ingredients in a small, heavy saucepan and stir over low heat until thoroughly combined.

Yield: About ½ cup.

Orange-Date Holiday Cake

The addition of oats and yogurt adds a new dimension to this old-fashioned cake.

3 cups all-purpose flour
1¼ cups uncooked old-fashioned
  rolled oats
3 teaspoons baking powder
1½ teaspoons baking soda
¼ teaspoon salt
1½ cups chopped pitted dates
1 cup chopped pecans
1 cup butter, softened

1¾ cups granulated sugar
4 eggs, lightly beaten
2 teaspoons vanilla extract
2 tablespoons grated orange peel
1¾ cups plain yogurt
Orange Syrup (recipe follows)
Orange slices, dates, and pecans,
  for garnish (optional)

1. Position rack in lower third of oven; preheat to 350°F. Grease a 10- by 4-inch tube pan or a 12-cup bundt pan; dust with flour.

2. In a medium bowl, whisk or stir together flour, oats, baking powder, baking soda, and salt. On a sheet of waxed paper, mix dates and pecans with 2 tablespoons dry ingredients; set aside.

3. In a large bowl, and using electric beaters, cream butter until light and smooth. Add sugar in several additions, beating until mixture is light and fluffy. Gradually add eggs, beating until mixture has the consistency of lightly whipped cream. Stir in vanilla and orange peel.

4. Using a large rubber spatula, alternately stir in dry ingredients and yogurt, beginning and ending with dry ingredients, and blending well after each addition. Stir in dates and walnuts. Pour batter into prepared pan, spreading evenly.

5. Bake 55 to 60 minutes, or until cake tester inserted in center comes out clean.

6. Prepare Orange Syrup.

7. When the cake is done, remove to wire rack. Immediately prick top of cake in several places with a toothpick. Slowly pour Orange Syrup over cake. Cool cake completely in pan, before loosening with a knife and removing. Wrap cake in plastic and refrigerate overnight. This cake looks especially pretty garnished with orange slices, dates, and pecans.

Yield: One 4- by 10-inch tube cake.

96

Orange Syrup

¾ cup freshly squeezed orange
  juice
⅔ cup granulated sugar

2 tablespoons freshly squeezed
  lemon juice
2 teaspoons grated orange peel

Heat all ingredients in a small saucepan until sugar dissolves.

Yield: ¾ cup.

Raisin and Nut Honey Cake

2⅓ cups all-purpose flour
1½ teaspoons baking powder
1 teaspoon baking soda
¼ teaspoon ground cloves
½ teaspoon ground ginger
½ teaspoon ground cinnamon
¼ teaspoon salt
½ cup golden raisins

1 cup chopped walnuts
2 eggs
⅔ cup granulated sugar
⅓ cup vegetable oil
1 cup honey
1 cup cold coffee
¼ cup mashed, ripe banana

1.   Position rack in center of oven; preheat to 350°F. Grease two 9- by 5- by 2¾-inch loaf pans; dust with flour.

2.   In a medium bowl, whisk or stir together flour, baking powder, baking soda, cloves, ginger, cinnamon, and salt. On a sheet of waxed paper, mix raisins and walnuts with 2 teaspoons dry ingredients; set aside.

3.   In a large bowl, and using electric beaters, beat eggs. Add sugar, 1 tablespoon at a time, beating until eggs are thick and lemon-colored (about 5 minutes). Reduce speed to lowest setting; slowly pour in oil, honey, and coffee, beating well after each addition. Stir in banana.

4.   Using a large rubber spatula, gradually add dry ingredients, stirring until completely blended. Stir in raisins and walnuts. Pour batter into prepared pans, dividing equally.

5.   Bake 55 to 60 minutes, or until cake tester inserted in center comes out clean. Remove pans to racks. Cool completely before loosening sides of cakes with a knife and removing from pans. Wrap snugly in plastic, and store in the refrigerator for 24 hours to allow flavors to develop. Serve at room temperature.

Yield: Two 9- by 5- by 2¾-inch loaves.

Apricot-Blueberry Loaf Cake

2 cups all-purpose flour
2 teaspoons baking powder
½ teaspoon baking soda
½ teaspoon ground cinnamon
½ teaspoon ground nutmeg
½ teaspoon ground cloves
½ teaspoon salt
2 cups fresh, or thawed, frozen
   blueberries

⅓ cup golden raisins
½ cup butter, softened
1 cup granulated sugar
3 eggs, lightly beaten
1 cup apricot preserves
⅓ cup buttermilk
Confectioners' sugar

1.   Position rack in center of oven; preheat to 350°F. Grease a 9- by 5- by 2¾-inch loaf pan; dust with flour.

2.   In a medium bowl, whisk or stir together flour, baking powder, baking soda, cinnamon, nutmeg, cloves, and salt. On a sheet of waxed paper, mix blueberries and raisins with 1 tablespoon dry ingredients; set aside.

3.   In a large bowl, and using electric beaters, cream butter until light and smooth. Add sugar in several additions, beating until mixture is light and fluffy. Gradually add eggs, beating until mixture has the consistency of lightly whipped cream. Stir in apricot preserves.

4.   Using a large rubber spatula, alternately stir in dry ingredients and buttermilk, beginning and ending with dry ingredients, and blending well after each addition. Carefully stir in blueberry-raisin mixture. Pour batter into prepared pan, spreading evenly.

5.   Bake 50 to 60 minutes, or until cake tester inserted in center comes out clean. Remove pan to wire rack. Cool 10 minutes before loosening cake from pan with a knife and removing. Finish cooling right side up on rack. Dust with confectioners' sugar just before serving.

Yield: One 9- by 5- by 2¾-inch loaf.

CAKE CUE

Buy blueberries that are plump and firm, with a light grayish bloom. Unwashed blueberries may be stored in the refrigerator for up to two weeks.

Old-Fashioned Strawberry Shortcake

Some people prefer their shortcake with a sponge-cake base. Either way, this American classic is delicious.

½ cup plus 3 tablespoons
  granulated sugar
1 quart fresh strawberries,
  washed, hulled, and sliced
2 cups flour
3 teaspoons baking powder

½ teaspoon salt
½ cup cold butter
¾ cup milk
2 tablespoons melted butter
Sweetened Whipped Cream (page
  156)

~~ ∞ ~~

C A K E   C U E

*Old-fashioned
shortcake isn't a
true cake at all, but
a pastry dough. The
term "short" refers
to shortening—
usually butter
or vegetable
shortening—in the
dough. Shortcake is
made with a high
proportion of
shortening and a
low proportion of
liquid in relation to
the amount of flour.
The fat coats the
protein molecules in
the flour and
prevents gluten from
forming. The result
is a light dough that
breaks or flakes
easily.*

1. In a large bowl, sprinkle the ½ cup sugar over strawberries and gently mix together. (Taste strawberries; if not sweet enough, add up to ¼ cup more sugar.) Refrigerate until needed.

2. Position rack in center of oven; preheat to 450°F. Lightly grease a 9-inch round cake pan.

3. In a medium bowl, whisk or stir together flour, the 3 tablespoons sugar, baking powder, and salt. Cut in the butter with a pastry blender or two knives until mixture resembles coarse crumbs. Gradually add milk, stirring with a fork just until mixture is moistened and begins to hold together. Knead dough briefly on lightly floured work surface; pat into prepared pan.

4. Bake 15 minutes, or until top is golden. Remove pan from oven and immediately remove cake from pan. Using a long serrated knife, split cake into two layers. Place bottom layer on a serving plate and spread cut surface with melted butter. Spoon on half the berry mixture, spreading berries to edge. Place next layer right side up on berries; pour remaining berries over top. Cut into wedges and serve with Sweetened Whipped Cream.

Yield: One 9-inch round cake.

Cupcakes and Cakes for Kids

Party Cupcakes

Kids love cupcakes, especially when they're frosted and decorated. Cupcakes are especially easy to serve at fairs, fund-raisers, and birthday parties because there's no fussing with cutting or serving.

Besides the cupcakes that follow on the next six pages, Yellow Layer Cake (page 31), Chocolate Layer Cake (page 30), and White Layer Cake (page 29) may also be baked as cupcakes. Bake the cupcakes in *paper-lined* tins; fill two-thirds full and bake in a preheated 350°F oven for 15 to 20 minutes or until cake tester inserted in center of one cupcake comes out clean. Cool cupcakes completely before frosting with Basic Buttercream Frosting (page 142), Fast Fudge Frosting (page 148), Sweetened Whipped Cream (page 156), or Cream Cheese Frosting (page 157).

To decorate cupcakes, choose from the following toppings.

- Lay three ½-inch pieces of red string licorice on top of frosting; crown each piece with M & M's® to resemble a bunch of balloons.
- Place a small plastic toy such as a dinosaur, doll, or cartoon character on each frosted cupcake.
- Toss sprinkles over frosting; insert a candy bear in center of frosting.
- For Halloween cupcakes, tint buttercream frosting with a few drops of orange food coloring; insert small plastic Halloween figures and surround with candy corn.
- Top cupcakes with sliced bananas; toss toasted coconut over banana slices, and crown with a cherry.

Black-Bottom Cupcakes

Topping

2 packages (3 ounces each) cream
  cheese, softened
¼ cup granulated sugar
1 egg, lightly beaten

¼ teaspoon salt
1 teaspoon grated orange peel
½ cup semisweet chocolate chips
¼ cup chopped peanuts

Cupcakes

1½ cups flour
⅔ cup granulated sugar
1 teaspoon baking soda
⅓ cup unsweetened cocoa powder
½ teaspoon salt

⅓ cup vegetable oil
1 cup buttermilk
1 teaspoon vanilla
½ cup semisweet chocolate chips

1. *To make topping:* Combine cream cheese, sugar, egg, salt, and orange peel in a small bowl. Beat with electric mixer until smooth and creamy. Stir in chocolate chips and peanuts; set aside.

2. Position rack in center of oven; preheat to 350°F. Grease twelve 3- by 1¼-inch muffin cups, or fill with paper liners.

3. *To make cupcakes:* In a large bowl, whisk or stir together flour, sugar, baking soda, cocoa, and salt. Add oil, buttermilk, and vanilla, and beat with a wire whisk until smooth. Stir in chocolate chips.

4. Fill prepared muffin cups two-thirds full with batter. Spoon 1½ tablespoons cream cheese topping over each cupcake.

5. Bake 20 minutes, or until cake tester inserted in center of one cupcake comes out clean. Remove tins to wire rack. Cool cupcakes in tins 5 minutes before removing; finish cooling on racks.

Yield: 12 cupcakes.

Butterfly Cupcakes

2 cups all-purpose flour
2 teaspoons baking powder
½ teaspoon salt
½ cup freshly squeezed orange
   juice
½ cup apricot preserves
2 teaspoons freshly squeezed
   lemon juice

½ cup butter
¾ cup granulated sugar
2 eggs, lightly beaten
½ recipe Basic Buttercream
   Frosting (page 142)
Confectioners' sugar

1.   Position rack in center of oven; preheat to 375°F. Fill eighteen 2½- by 1¼-inch cupcake tins with paper liners. (Fill unused tins with ¼ cup water to prevent scorching.)

2.   In a medium bowl, whisk or stir together flour, baking powder, and salt; set aside. Combine orange juice, apricot preserves, and lemon juice in a measuring cup; set aside.

3.   In a large bowl, and using electric beaters, cream butter until light and smooth. Add sugar in several additions, beating until mixture is light and fluffy. Gradually add eggs, beating until mixture has the consistency of lightly whipped cream.

4.   Using a large rubber spatula, alternately stir in dry ingredients and orange juice mixture, beginning and ending with dry ingredients, and blending well after each addition. Fill prepared muffin cups two-thirds full with batter.

5.   Bake 20 to 25 minutes, or until cake tester inserted in center of one cupcake comes out clean. Remove tins to wire racks. Cool cupcakes in tins 5 minutes before removing; finish cooling on racks.

6.   *To decorate cupcakes:* With a sharp knife, cut top off each cupcake right above paper liner. You now have eighteen circles. Cut each circle in half crosswise. Spoon about 1 tablespoon buttercream over cupcakes. Position two half-tops on buttercream, pressing them lightly to form a **V** shape representing the wings of the butterfly; dust with confectioners' sugar. Spoon a small amount of buttercream into the **V** to form the body of the butterfly.

Yield: 18 cupcakes.

Mocha-Spice Cupcakes with Orange Sun-Kissed Frosting

2 cups all-purpose flour
2 teaspoons baking powder
½ teaspoon baking soda
2 tablespoons unsweetened cocoa
   powder
1 teaspoon instant-coffee powder
½ teaspoon salt
1 teaspoon ground cinnamon
¼ teaspoon ground nutmeg
¼ teaspoon ground cloves

½ cup butter, softened
1 cup firmly packed light brown
   sugar
3 eggs, lightly beaten
⅔ cup buttermilk
Orange Sun-Kissed Frosting
   (recipe follows)
1 square (1 ounce) semisweet
   chocolate, grated

1.   Position rack in center of oven; preheat to 375°F. Grease twelve 3- by 1¼-inch muffin cups, or fill with paper liners.

2.   In a medium bowl, whisk or stir together flour, baking powder, baking soda, cocoa powder, coffee powder, salt, cinnamon, nutmeg, and cloves; set aside.

3.   In a large bowl, and using electric beaters, cream butter until light and smooth. Add sugar in several additions, beating until mixture is light and fluffy. Add dry ingredients, eggs, and buttermilk; beat until smooth and well blended. Fill prepared muffin cups two-thirds full with batter.

4.   Bake 15 to 20 minutes, or until cake tester inserted in center of one cupcake comes out clean. Remove tins to wire rack. Cool cupcakes in tins 5 minutes before removing; finish cooling on racks.

5.   Make Orange Sun-Kissed Frosting. Spread frosting on cupcakes and sprinkle with grated chocolate.

Yield: 12 cupcakes.

Orange Sun-Kissed Frosting

¼ *cup butter, softened*
1½ *tablespoons finely grated*
    orange peel
2 *tablespoons freshly squeezed*
    orange juice
1¾ *cups sifted confectioners'*
    sugar

In a small bowl, cream butter, orange peel, and orange juice until light and fluffy. Add confectioners' sugar gradually, beating until well blended.

Yield: About 1 cup.

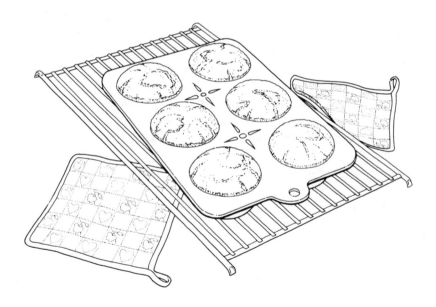

Peanut Butter Cupcakes with Crunchy Topping

Cupcakes

2 cups all-purpose flour
1¼ cups firmly packed light
* brown sugar*
3 teaspoons baking powder
1 cup milk

⅓ cup vegetable oil
⅔ cup chunky peanut butter
2 eggs, lightly beaten
1½ teaspoons vanilla extract

Topping

½ cup miniature semisweet
* chocolate chips*

½ cup chopped peanuts
⅓ cup flaked coconut

1. Position rack in center of oven; preheat to 375°F. Grease eighteen 3- by 1¼-inch muffin cups, or fill with paper liners. (Fill unused tins halfway with water to prevent scorching.)

2. *To make cupcakes:* In a large bowl, whisk or stir together flour, sugar, and baking powder. Make a well in the center; add milk, oil, peanut butter, eggs, and vanilla, and beat until smooth and well blended. Fill muffin cups two-thirds full with batter.

3. *To make topping:* Combine chocolate chips, peanuts, and coconut; sprinkle over cupcakes, dividing evenly.

4. Bake 20 minutes, or until cake tester inserted in center of one cupcake comes out clean. Remove tins to wire racks. Cool cupcakes in tins 5 minutes before removing. Finish cooling on racks.

Yield: 18 cupcakes.

Orange Juice Cake

1⅓ cups all-purpose flour
1 teaspoon baking powder
¼ teaspoon salt
1 cup currants
½ cup butter
¾ cup granulated sugar

2 eggs, lightly beaten
1 tablespoon finely grated orange
 peel
¼ cup freshly squeezed orange
 juice

1. Position rack in center of oven; preheat to 350°F. Grease an 8-inch square cake pan; dust with flour.

2. In a medium bowl, whisk or stir together flour, baking powder, and salt. On a sheet of waxed paper, mix currants with 1 teaspoon dry ingredients; set aside.

3. In a large bowl, and using electric beaters, cream butter until light and smooth. Add sugar in several additions, beating until mixture is light and fluffy. Gradually add eggs, beating until mixture has the consistency of lightly whipped cream. Stir in orange peel.

4. Using a large rubber spatula, alternately stir in dry ingredients and orange juice, beginning and ending with dry ingredients, and blending well after each addition. Stir in currants. Pour batter into prepared pan, spreading evenly.

5. Bake 35 minutes, or until cake tester inserted in center comes out clean. Remove pan to wire rack. Cool 10 minutes before loosening cake from pan with a knife and removing. Finish cooling right side up on rack.

Yield: One 8-inch square cake.

Crazy Cake

6 tablespoons butter
1½ cups all-purpose flour
1 cup granulated sugar
¼ cup plus 2 tablespoons
    unsweetened cocoa powder
1 teaspoon baking soda

¼ teaspoon salt
1 tablespoon cider vinegar
1½ teaspoons vanilla extract
1 cup milk
Frosting of choice or whipped
    cream (optional)

1.   Position rack in center of oven; preheat to 350°F. Grease an 8-inch square pan; dust with flour.

2.   In a small saucepan, melt butter; set aside. In a medium bowl, whisk or stir together flour, sugar, cocoa powder, baking soda, and salt. Using the back of a spoon, make three small indentations in dry ingredients; pour melted butter into the first, vinegar into the second, and vanilla into the third. Pour milk over mixture and beat with a fork until dark, smooth, and well blended. Pour batter into prepared pan, spreading evenly.

3.   Bake 25 to 30 minutes, or until cake tester inserted in center comes out clean. Remove pan to wire rack. Cool 10 minutes before loosening cake from pan with a knife and removing. Finish cooling right side up on rack. Serve plain, with your favorite frosting, or with whipped cream.

Yield: One 8-inch square cake.

Mom's Chocolate-Pudding Refrigerator Cake

¼ cup cornstarch
3 cups milk
½ cup granulated sugar
3 squares (3 ounces) semisweet
  chocolate
Pinch salt
¼ teaspoon vanilla extract

1 tablespoon butter
27 square cinnamon-flavored
  graham crackers
1 cup heavy cream
Chocolate curls (page 20) or
  grated chocolate (optional)

1. Line the bottom of an 8-inch square cake pan with aluminum foil, allowing ends of foil to extend about 2 inches over sides of pan.

2. In a medium saucepan over low heat, combine cornstarch, milk, sugar, chocolate, and salt. Bring to a gentle boil, stirring constantly until chocolate melts and mixture is smooth, dark, and coats the back of a spoon (about 5 minutes). Remove from heat; stir in vanilla and butter.

3. Arrange 9 crackers on bottom of pan; pour in one third of the chocolate pudding, spreading evenly. Arrange 9 crackers over pudding; pour in one half of the remaining pudding, spreading evenly. Arrange remaining crackers on top; pour remaining pudding over crackers, spreading evenly. Cool 10 minutes. Cover loosely with aluminum foil or plastic wrap to allow steam to escape, and refrigerate at least 3 hours. Using the ends of foil as handles, lift cake and transfer to serving platter.

4. In a medium bowl, and using electric beaters, beat cream until thick. Spread on top of cake; decorate with chocolate curls or grated chocolate, if desired.

Yield: One 8-inch square cake.

Cheesecakes and Pudding Cakes

CHEESECAKE

"Put as much wine to a quart of milk as will turn it well—
put 2 or 3 eggs into the milk before you boil it. When turned,
skim off the whey, add some butter, currants and as much
sugar as you like; if you wish them white, leave out the
yolks."

—Handwritten recipe, circa 1850

Old New York Cheesecake

Crust

4 tablespoons butter
2⅓ cups graham cracker crumbs
  (about 16 whole crackers)

2 tablespoons granulated sugar
¼ teaspoon ground cinnamon

Cheesecake

1½ pounds cream cheese,
  softened
1½ cups granulated sugar
1 teaspoon vanilla extract

3 tablespoons freshly squeezed
  lemon juice
3 eggs
2 cups sour cream

1. Position rack in lower third of oven; preheat to 325°F. Lightly oil a 9-inch springform pan.

2. *To make crust:* In a medium saucepan, melt butter; cool slightly. Add cracker crumbs, sugar, and cinnamon; combine thoroughly. Using the back of a spoon, press mixture evenly over bottom and partly up sides of prepared pan. Bake 5 minutes. Cool on wire rack.

3. *To make cheesecake:* In a large bowl, and using electric beaters set on high speed, beat cream cheese and sugar until very smooth and light (about 10 minutes), stopping frequently to scrape down bottom and sides of bowl. Beat in vanilla and lemon juice. Reduce speed to lowest setting; add eggs, one at a time, beating only until blended. Stir in sour cream. Pour mixture into prepared pan, spreading evenly.

4. Bake 1 hour, or until cake is firm. Turn off the oven. Using a pot holder, prop open oven door and leave cheesecake in oven for 1 hour. At the end of 1 hour, open oven door and touch top of cake; it should feel dry and barely warm. (If it feels hot, close door and leave cake in oven for another hour.) Remove cake from oven.

5. Run a knife around sides of cake to loosen it from pan; release and remove sides of pan. Leave cheesecake on bottom of pan and place it on a wire rack to cool completely. Cover with plastic wrap and refrigerate until cold. Slide a long metal spatula under crust to loosen it from bottom of pan; transfer cake to a serving platter. Serve at room temperature.

Yield: One 9-inch cheesecake.

Pistachio Cheesecake

Crust

¼ cup butter
½ cup shelled and skinned
  pistachios (preferably undyed)

10 whole graham crackers
2 tablespoons granulated sugar

Cheesecake

1½ pounds cream cheese,
  softened
1 cup granulated sugar
2 tablespoons all-purpose flour
2 teaspoons vanilla extract
¼ cup heavy cream

3 eggs
1½ cups chopped, shelled, and
  skinned pistachios (preferably
  undyed)
¼ cup apricot preserves

1. Position rack in center of oven; preheat oven to 350°F. Lightly oil an 8-inch springform pan.

2. *To make crust:* In a small saucepan, melt butter; set aside. Combine pistachios and graham crackers in a blender or the bowl of a food processor, and process until finely chopped. Add sugar and butter and process just until combined. Using the back of a tablespoon, press crumb crust over bottom and partly up sides of prepared pan. Bake 10 minutes. Remove to wire rack.

3. *To make cheesecake:* In a large bowl, and using electric beaters, beat cream cheese and sugar until very light and smooth (about 10 minutes), stopping frequently to scrape down bottom and sides of bowl. Beat in flour, vanilla, and heavy cream until well blended. Reduce speed to lowest setting; add eggs, one at a time, beating only until blended. Stir in 1 cup of the pistachios. Pour mixture into prepared pan, spreading top with a spatula.

4. Bake 1 hour, or until top is firm and lightly browned. Turn off oven. Using a pot holder, prop open oven door and leave cheesecake in oven for 1 hour. At the end of 1 hour, open oven door and touch top of cake; it should feel dry and barely warm. (If it feels hot, close door and leave cake in oven for another hour.) Remove cake from oven.

5.   Run a knife around sides of cake to loosen it from pan; release and remove sides of pan. Leave cheesecake on bottom of pan and place it on a wire rack to cool completely. Cover with plastic wrap and refrigerate until cold. Slide a long metal spatula under crust to loosen it from bottom of pan; transfer cake to a serving platter.

6.   Heat apricot preserves in a small, heavy saucepan over low heat, stirring constantly, until softened; spread preserves evenly over top of cheesecake. Sprinkle remaining ½ cup chopped nuts decoratively over top. Serve at room temperature.

Yield: One 8-inch cheesecake.

Chocolate Chip–Marble Cheesecake

Crust

4 tablespoons butter
1 cup finely crushed chocolate
  wafers (18 to 20 wafers)

½ cup finely chopped walnuts
2 tablespoons granulated sugar

Cheesecake

2 pounds cream cheese, softened
1¼ cups granulated sugar
2 teaspoons vanilla extract
4 eggs, lightly beaten
1½ cups sour cream

4 squares (4 ounces) semisweet
  chocolate, melted and cooled
2 squares (2 ounces) semisweet
  chocolate, coarsely chopped

1. Position rack in lower third of oven; preheat to 325°F. Lightly oil a 9-inch springform pan.

2. *To make crust:* In a small saucepan, melt butter. In a small bowl, mix together crushed wafers, chopped walnuts, and sugar; stir in melted butter. Using the back of a spoon, press mixture into bottom of pan evenly. Refrigerate until needed.

3. *To make cheesecake:* In a large mixing bowl, and using beaters set on high speed, beat cream cheese and sugar until very light and smooth (about 10 minutes), stopping frequently to scrape down bottom and sides of bowl. Beat in vanilla. Reduce speed to lowest setting; add eggs, one at a time, beating only until blended. Stir in sour cream.

4. Transfer one half of the batter to a medium bowl; add cooled chocolate, stirring until well blended. Add chopped chocolate to remaining batter, stirring until well blended. Fill prepared pan, alternating spoonfuls of light batter with spoonfuls of chocolate batter. Draw a narrow spatula or knife through the batter to form the marbling.

5. Bake 1¼ hours, or until cake is firm. Turn off oven. Using a pot holder, prop open oven door and leave cheesecake in oven for 1 hour. At the end of 1 hour, open oven door and touch top of cake; it should feel dry and barely warm. (If it feels hot, close door and leave cake in oven for another hour.) Remove cake from oven.

6. Run a knife around sides of cake to loosen it from pan; release and remove sides of pan. Leave cheesecake on bottom of pan and place it on a wire rack to finish cooling completely. Cover with plastic wrap and refrigerate until cold. Slide a long metal spatula under crust to loosen it from bottom of pan; transfer cake to a serving platter. Serve at room temperature.

Yield: One 9-inch cheesecake.

Lemon Pudding Cake

This dessert is delicious and virtually fail-proof.

¼ cup all-purpose flour
1 cup plus 2 tablespoons
   granulated sugar
¼ teaspoon salt
3 eggs, separated

1½ cups milk
¼ cup freshly squeezed lemon
   juice
1 teaspoon grated lemon peel
Vanilla ice cream (optional)

   1.   Position rack in center of oven; preheat to 350°F. Have ready an un-greased 1-quart baking dish for the pudding cake and a slightly larger, shallow pan filled with 1 to 2 inches of hot water.

   2.   In a medium bowl, whisk or stir together flour, the 1 cup sugar, and salt; set aside.

   3.   In another medium bowl, beat egg yolks with a fork until blended; stir in milk, lemon juice, and peel. Stir yolk mixture into dry ingredients, blending well.

   4.   In a separate bowl, and using electric beaters, beat egg whites until soft peaks form. Add the 2 tablespoons sugar and beat until whites stand in stiff, moist, shiny peaks. Carefully fold whites into yolk mixture. Pour batter into ungreased baking dish, then set in pan of water. Place pans in oven and bake pudding until set and top is well browned (about 40 minutes). Sauce will form under cake. Remove pan to a wire rack and cool 15 minutes before serving.

   5.   To serve, use a large spoon to transfer cake and sauce to dessert dishes. This cake is delicious as is, or with a scoop of vanilla ice cream.

Yield: 6 to 8 servings.

Hot Fudge Upside-Down Cake

Freeze the leftovers from this recipe and eat them straight from the freezer, or cut them up and stir into vanilla ice cream. Heavenly!

1 cup all-purpose flour
2 teaspoons baking powder
1 cup granulated sugar
¼ teaspoon salt
3 tablespoons plus ¼ cup
   unsweetened cocoa powder
½ cup milk
4 tablespoons butter, melted and
   cooled

1 teaspoon vanilla extract
¾ cup firmly packed dark brown
   sugar
1¾ cups very hot water
Sweetened Whipped Cream (page
   156, optional)

1. Position rack in center of oven; preheat to 350°F. Have ready an ungreased 9-inch square baking pan.
2. In a medium bowl, whisk or stir together flour, baking powder, ¾ cup of the granulated sugar, salt, and the 3 tablespoons cocoa. Add milk, butter, and vanilla, stirring until mixture is smooth, dark, and well blended. Pour batter into ungreased pan.
3. In a small bowl, whisk together brown sugar, remaining ¼ cup granulated sugar, and remaining ¼ cup cocoa. Sprinkle evenly over batter. Pour the hot water over batter, but *do not stir together.*
4. Bake 40 minutes. Mixture will form both a cake and a sauce in the pan. Remove pan to wire rack. Cool 15 minutes before serving. Serve warm, either plain or with whipped cream.

Yield: One 9-inch square cake.

Modern-Day Classic Cakes and Special-Occasion Cakes

OLD-FASHIONED WEDDING CAKE

"Five pounds each of flour, butter, and sugar, six of raisins, twelve of currants, two of citron, fifty eggs, half a pint of good Málaga wine, three ounces of nutmegs, three of cinnamon, one and a half of mace. Bake in three large pans four hours."

—*The Young Housekeeper's Friend,*
by Mrs. Cornelous, 1859

Zucchini-Almond Loaf Cake

Whole wheat pastry flour combined with regular whole wheat flour makes this cake light and airy.

3 egg whites, lightly beaten
1 cup firmly packed light brown
    sugar
1 cup safflower oil
½ cup honey
⅓ cup freshly squeezed lemon
    juice
1 tablespoon finely grated lemon
    peel

1½ cups whole wheat flour
1 cup whole wheat pastry flour
2 teaspoons baking powder
½ teaspoon baking soda
½ teaspoon salt
1 cup chopped, unblanched
    almonds
2 cups unpeeled, shredded
    zucchini

1.   Position rack in center of oven; preheat to 350°F. Grease two 8½- by 4½- by 2½-inch loaf pans; dust with flour.

2.   In a large bowl, and using a fork, beat together egg whites, sugar, oil, honey, lemon juice, and peel until well blended.

3.   In a medium bowl, whisk or stir together flours, baking powder, baking soda, and salt; stir into oil mixture ½ cup at a time until well blended. Stir in almonds and zucchini. Pour batter into prepared pan, spreading evenly.

4.   Bake 50 minutes, or until cake tester inserted in center comes out clean. Remove pans to wire racks. Cool 10 minutes before loosening cakes from pans with a knife and removing. Finish cooling right side up on racks.

Yield: Two 8½- by 4½- by 2½-inch loaves.

California Fruit and Nut Cake

2 cups unbleached all-purpose
  flour
1 teaspoon baking powder
½ teaspoon baking soda
¼ teaspoon ground cinnamon
¼ teaspoon salt
1 cup soy margarine (available at
  most health-food stores)
¾ cup honey
2 eggs, lightly beaten
1 teaspoon vanilla extract
¾ cup plain yogurt
¼ cup chopped unblanched
  almonds

¼ cup chopped pecans
¼ cup chopped pistachios
  (preferably undyed)
¼ cup chopped pitted dates
¼ cup chopped dried calmyrna
  figs (available in health food
  stores)
¼ cup chopped dried papaya
1 tablespoon carob powder
½ cup sweetened carob chips
Carob Glaze (recipe follows)

CAKE CUE

*Before chopping
dried fruits, dip
knife or scissors in
warm water to
prevent sticking.*

1. Position rack in lower third of oven; preheat to 325°F. Grease a 12-cup bundt pan; dust with flour.

2. In a medium bowl, whisk or stir together flour, baking powder, baking soda, cinnamon, and salt.

3. In a large bowl, and using electric beaters, cream soy margarine until light and smooth. Slowly pour in honey, beating until well blended. Gradually add eggs, beating until mixture has the consistency of lightly whipped cream. Stir in vanilla.

4. Using a large rubber spatula, alternately stir in dry ingredients, and yogurt, beginning and ending with dry ingredients, and blending well after each addition.

5. On a sheet of waxed paper, mix nuts and fruits with carob powder until lightly coated; stir into batter. Stir in carob chips. Pour batter into prepared pan, spreading evenly.

6. Bake 60 to 65 minutes, or until cake tester inserted in center comes out clean. Remove pan to wire rack. Cool 10 minutes before removing from pan; finish cooling on rack. Pour Carob Glaze over top of cake, letting it run down sides.

Yield: One 12-cup bundt cake.

Carob Glaze

3 tablespoons carob powder
2 tablespoons plain yogurt
¼ cup honey

In a small bowl, stir together carob powder, yogurt, and honey until well blended.

Yield: About ⅓ cup.

Banana-Blueberry Buckle

Topping

1 cup granola
½ cup firmly packed brown sugar

½ teaspoon ground cinnamon
⅓ cup soy margarine

Cake

2 cups whole wheat pastry flour
2 teaspoons baking powder
¼ teaspoon ground nutmeg
½ teaspoon salt
2 cups fresh or thawed, frozen
   blueberries
½ cup soy margarine

¾ cup firmly packed light brown
   sugar
1 egg, lightly beaten
1 teaspoon vanilla extract
1 cup mashed ripe banana
½ cup chopped walnuts

1. Position rack in center of oven; preheat to 375°F. Line a 9-inch square pan with aluminum foil so that ends of foil extend 2 inches beyond pan; fold ends under pan; grease; dust with flour.

2. *To make topping:* In a small bowl, combine granola, sugar, and cinnamon. Cut in margarine until mixture resembles coarse crumbs; set aside.

3. *To make cake:* In a medium bowl, whisk or stir together flour, baking powder, nutmeg, and salt. On a sheet of waxed paper, mix 2 teaspoons dry ingredients with blueberries; set aside.

4. In a large bowl, and using electric beaters, cream margarine until light and smooth. Add sugar in several additions, beating until mixture is light and fluffy. Gradually add egg, beating until mixture has the consistency of lightly whipped cream. Stir in vanilla.

5. Using a large rubber spatula, alternately stir in dry ingredients and mashed banana, beginning and ending with dry ingredients, and blending well after each addition. Carefully fold in blueberries. Pour batter into prepared pan, spreading evenly. Toss walnuts over top, then sprinkle crumb topping evenly over batter.

128

6. Bake 45 minutes, or until top is lightly browned. Remove pan to wire rack and cool 30 minutes. Using ends of foil as handles, lift cake from pan and transfer to serving platter before cutting into squares. Serve warm or at room temperature.

Yield: One 9-inch square cake.

Dried Apple and Molasses Cake

1 cup firmly packed, chopped
  dried apples
2¼ cups whole wheat pastry flour
1 teaspoon baking powder
1 teaspoon baking soda
1 teaspoon ground cinnamon
½ teaspoon ground cloves
½ teaspoon salt
½ cup dark molasses

2 egg whites, lightly beaten
½ cup firmly packed light brown
  sugar
½ cup safflower oil
1 cup plain yogurt
1 teaspoon finely grated orange
  peel
½ cup chopped walnuts

1. In a small saucepan, combine dried apples and ½ cup water; cover and bring to a boil over moderate heat. Reduce heat to low and simmer gently 15 minutes. Remove from heat; set aside, still covered, until needed.

2. Position rack in center of oven; preheat to 350°F. Line a 9-inch square pan with aluminum foil so that ends of foil extend 2 inches over sides of pan; grease; dust with flour.

3. In a medium bowl, whisk or stir together flour, baking powder, baking soda, cinnamon, cloves, and salt.

4. In a large bowl, and using a fork, beat together molasses, egg whites, sugar, oil, yogurt, and orange peel until well blended. Stir in dry ingredients, ¼ cup at a time, blending well after each addition. Stir in apples and chopped walnuts. Pour batter into prepared pan, spreading evenly.

5. Bake 25 to 30 minutes, or until cake tester inverted in center comes out clean. Remove pan to wire rack and cool 10 minutes. Using foil ends as handles, lift cake and place on wire rack to finish cooling.

Yield: One 9-inch square cake.

No-Cheese Cheesecake

Crust

1 cup crushed honey-flavored
graham crackers (about 9
whole crackers)

3 tablespoons soy margarine,
melted

Filling

2 pounds firm tofu
½ cup pure maple syrup
2 eggs

1 teaspoon vanilla extract
¼ teaspoon salt
¼ cup carob powder

1. Position rack in center of oven; preheat to 350°F. Lightly oil an 8-inch springform pan.

2. *To make crust:* In a small bowl, combine crackers and soy margarine until crackers are completely moistened. Using the back of a tablespoon, press mixture firmly into bottom of oiled pan; bake 5 minutes.

3. *To make filling:* In a large bowl, and using electric beaters, beat tofu on high speed until smooth. Add maple syrup, eggs, vanilla, salt, and carob powder; beat until well blended. Pour mixture into pan, smoothing top with a rubber spatula.

4. Bake 30 minutes, or until cake is set. Using a pot holder, prop open oven door and leave cheesecake in oven for 30 minutes. Remove pan to wire rack and cool completely. Cover cake with aluminum foil or plastic wrap, and refrigerate at least 2 hours before serving.

Yield: One 8-inch cheesecake.

Simple Tiered Wedding Cake

This sponge cake is delicious and relatively easy to make. You'll need a *5-quart heavy-duty mixer* to whip up *two separate batches* of batter. Bake the 12-inch layers first, then prepare *second batch of the batter*, and bake the 10- and 8-inch layers. It's important to make the batter in *separate* batches; otherwise the baking powder would lose its leavening power while waiting to go into the oven. If you take your time and follow the directions carefully, this cake is a snap to make.

Cake Batter

10 *whole eggs*
5 *egg yolks*
1¼ *cups granulated sugar*

¼ *teaspoon salt*
2½ *cups sifted cake flour*
1 *teaspoon baking powder*

Sugar Syrup

2¼ *cups water*
1¼ *cups granulated sugar*
3 *tablespoons Grand Marnier*

Coated Almonds

2 *pounds sliced almonds*
2 *egg whites*
4 *cups granulated sugar*

Grand Marnier Buttercream

8 *egg whites, at room*
   temperature
2½ *cups granulated sugar*
Pinch *salt*

4½ *cups butter, softened (9*
   sticks)
¼ *cup Grand Marnier*

Decoration

Miniature roses
Baby's breath

1.   *To make tiers:* Position rack in center of oven; preheat to 350°F. Grease two 12- by 2-inch round cake pans; line with waxed paper; grease; dust with flour.

2.   In the 5-quart bowl of a heavy-duty electric mixer, combine eggs, yolks, sugar, and salt. Set bowl over hot, not simmering, water, and whisk egg mixture constantly until sugar dissolves and mixture is lukewarm.

3.   Transfer bowl to electric mixer; beat on highest speed until mixture is cool and increases in volume (about 5 minutes).

4.   In the meantime, combine flour and baking powder, and sift once. When egg mixture is ready, remove bowl from stand. Sift dry ingredients over egg mixture in four or five additions, folding gently but thoroughly after each addition. Pour batter into prepared pans, dividing equally. Tilt pans in one direction to form a thin coat of batter on inside wall of each pan. Gently tap pans on work surface two or three times to remove any large air bubbles.

5.   Bake 35 to 40 minutes, or until center of cake springs back when lightly pressed. Remove pans to wire racks. Run a knife around edges of layers to loosen; invert immediately onto a wire rack and carefully peel off waxed paper. Place paper loosely on layers and invert onto other racks; finish cooling right side up. Cool completely; wrap in plastic and refrigerate overnight.

6.   Position two racks to divide oven into thirds. Prepare two 10- by 2-inch round cake pans and two 8- by 2-inch round cake pans as directed in Step 1. Prepare batter exactly as described in Step 2 through Step 4. There will be enough batter to fill each pan a little more than half full. Tilt pans in one direction to form a thin coat of batter on inside wall of each pan. Gently tap pans on work surface two or three times to remove any large air bubbles.

7.   Bake 25 to 30 minutes, or until center of cake springs back when lightly pressed. Remove pans to wire racks. Run a knife around edges of layers to loosen; invert immediately onto a wire rack and carefully peel off waxed paper. Place paper loosely on layers and invert onto other racks; finish cooling right side up. Cool completely; wrap in plastic and refrigerate overnight.

8.   *To make sugar syrup:* In a large saucepan, combine the water and sugar; bring to a boil over medium heat, stirring occasionally. Remove from heat; stir in Grand Marnier. Cover; store at room temperature.

9.   *To make coated almonds:* Place sliced almonds in a pan large enough to hold them in a layer no more than 1 inch deep. Pour on enough egg white just to dampen. Toss sugar over nuts and stir until sugar clings to nuts evenly. Bake

133

in a preheated 325°F oven about 30 minutes, stirring every 5 minutes. When done, nuts will have a coating of sugar clinging to them.

10. *To make buttercream:* In the 5-quart bowl of a heavy-duty electric mixer, combine egg whites, sugar, and salt. Set bowl over hot, not simmering, water and whisk mixture constantly until white, creamy, and hot to the touch. Rub a small bit of the mixture between your thumb and forefinger to make sure sugar crystals are completely dissolved.

11. Transfer bowl to electric mixer; beat mixture at medium-high speed until it is cool and thick (about 15 to 20 minutes). Add butter, 1 tablespoon at a time, beating after each addition until each piece is incorporated and butter is thick and smooth. Beat in Grand Marnier.

12. *To assemble separate tiers:* Put a dab of buttercream in center of an 8-inch cardboard circle and set one 8-inch layer on top, bottom side down. Using a pastry brush, brush layer with sugar syrup. Spread ¾ cup buttercream on layer; place second 8-inch layer on top of buttercream, bottom side up. Brush with sugar syrup. Assemble 10-inch and 12-inch layers, using a 10-inch cardboard circle and a 12-inch circle, respectively, as described above. Use 1 cup buttercream for 10-inch layer and 1¼ cups buttercream for 12-inch layer.

13. *To frost cakes:* Set first cake to be frosted on a cake turntable or on an inverted cake pan of the same size. Using a metal spatula, frost sides and then top with a thin layer of buttercream to help seal any loose crumbs. Refrigerate 5 minutes to harden. Apply a second, thicker layer to cake. To smooth top, hold cake spatula upright on edge of cake; pull spatula toward you, straight across cake. Return excess icing to bowl. Smooth sides by holding spatula upright, with tip at base of cake. To achieve a super-smooth finish, place spatula in very hot water for 1 minute and wipe off. Set blade flat against top of cake and slowly spin cake around. Heat spatula once again; wipe off. Hold flat side of blade against side of cake; spin to smooth entire side. Repeat procedure with remaining cakes.

14. Gently press some of the coated almonds into sides of each cake so that sides are completely covered. Remaining almonds will be used later to cover tops of cakes.

15. *To assemble finished cake:* To stack layers, start by placing the 12-inch cake on a 14-inch round serving plate. Center an 8-inch cardboard cake circle on cake to define a circle. Remove and insert six drinking straws, cut to height of cake, along inside edge of circle. Carefully stack the 10-inch cake on top, centering it. Press a small plate, 4 or 5 inches in diameter, on top of the 10-inch cake to define a circle. Remove plate and insert three drinking straws, cut to height of cake, inside circle. Carefully stack the 8-inch cake on top, centering it. Sprinkle an even layer of sugared almonds over top of each cake.

16. Decorate base of each cake with miniature roses and baby's breath, or flowers of your choice.

Yield: One 3-tiered wedding cake, enough for 50 to 55 servings.

Groom's Cake
(Banana–Chocolate-Chunk Rum Cake)

Traditionally, Groom's Cake is cut into small pieces and given to guests to put under their pillows. Whomever each dreams about that night is the person he or she will marry!

Unsweetened cocoa powder
2¼ cups all-purpose flour
2 teaspoons instant-coffee powder
½ cup unsweetened cocoa powder
2 teaspoons baking powder
½ teaspoon baking soda
½ teaspoon salt
1 cup butter, softened

1½ cups granulated sugar
4 eggs, lightly beaten
¼ cup light or dark rum
1½ cups mashed, ripe banana
12 squares (12 ounces) semisweet
   chocolate, coarsely chopped
Confectioners' sugar

1. Position rack in center of oven; preheat to 350°F. Grease a 9- by 13-inch baking pan; dust with cocoa powder.
2. In a medium bowl, whisk or stir together flour, coffee powder, cocoa powder, baking powder, baking soda, and salt; set aside.
3. In a large bowl, and using electric beaters, cream butter until light and smooth. Add granulated sugar in several additions, beating until mixture is light and fluffy. Gradually add eggs, beating until the mixture has the consistency of lightly whipped cream.
4. Using a large rubber spatula, alternately add the combined dry ingredients, rum, and mashed banana, beginning and ending with dry ingredients, and blending well after each addition. Fold in chocolate. Spoon batter into prepared pan, spreading evenly.
5. Bake 55 to 60 minutes, or until cake springs back when lightly pressed in center. Cool in pan 10 minutes; invert onto wire rack. Invert immediately onto another wire rack to cool completely. Dust with confectioners' sugar just before serving.

Yield: One 9- by 13-inch cake (35 servings, if cut into small pieces).

135

Frostings, Fillings, and Glazes

Simple Sugar Glaze with Two Variations

This glaze is a welcomed addition to almost any plain cake.

1 cup confectioners' sugar
2 tablespoons milk

1 tablespoon freshly squeezed
lemon juice

In a small bowl, and using electric beaters, combine all ingredients and beat until smooth. Glaze should be thick, but pourable. If it's too thick, add another tablespoon of milk.

Yield: About ½ cup.

Lemon Glaze: Omit milk; substitute 2 tablespoons freshly squeezed lemon juice and 1 teaspoon grated lemon peel.

Orange Glaze: Omit milk and lemon juice; substitute 4 tablespoons freshly squeezed orange juice and 1 teaspoon grated orange peel.

7-Minute Frosting

You need an old-fashioned, hand-held rotary beater or portable electric beaters to make this frosting.

3 egg whites
1½ cups granulated sugar
¼ cup water
Pinch salt

⅛ teaspoon cream of tartar
2 teaspoons light corn syrup
2 teaspoons vanilla extract

1. In the top part of a double boiler, combine egg whites, sugar, the water, salt, cream of tartar, and corn syrup; beat until blended (about 1 minute).
2. Place over boiling water, beating constantly for 7 minutes, or until soft peaks form when beater is slowly lifted.
3. Remove pan from boiling water; add vanilla and continue beating until frosting is cool and thick enough to spread (about 7 minutes).

Yield: Enough to fill and frost an 8- or 9-inch 2-layer cake, or to frost a 10-inch tube cake or a 9- by 13- by 2-inch cake.

Chocolate–Sour Cream Frosting

14 squares (14 ounces) semisweet
   chocolate
1¼ cups sour cream

1 teaspoon vanilla extract
Pinch salt

In the top part of a double boiler, melt chocolate over simmering water. Remove pan from water. Add sour cream, vanilla, and salt, and beat with a wire whisk until mixture is creamy and spreads easily. Frosting will harden as it cools.

Yield: Enough to fill and frost an 8- or 9-inch 2-layer cake, or to frost a 10-inch tube cake or a 9- by 13- by 2-inch cake.

Basic Buttercream Frosting and Three Variations

¾ cup butter, softened
3¼ cups sifted confectioners'
sugar

1½ teaspoons vanilla extract
2 to 3 tablespoons milk

In a medium bowl, and using electric beaters, cream butter until light and smooth. Add sugar, ½ cup at a time, beating until mixture is very creamy and smooth. Beat in vanilla and 2 tablespoons of the milk. If frosting seems too thick to spread, beat in additional tablespoon of milk.

Yield: Enough to fill and frost an 8- or 9-inch 2-layer cake, or to frost a 10-inch tube cake or a 9- by 13- by 2-inch cake.

Chocolate Buttercream Frosting: Beat in 3 tablespoons unsweetened cocoa powder or 2 squares (2 ounces) melted unsweetened chocolate before adding vanilla; increase milk to 3 or 4 tablespoons.

Lemon Buttercream Frosting: Omit vanilla and milk; substitute 2 tablespoons lemon juice and 1 teaspoon grated lemon peel.

Almond Buttercream Frosting: Omit vanilla; substitute ½ teaspoon almond extract.

Coconut Cream Filling

¼ cup granulated sugar
2 tablespoons cornstarch
Pinch salt
1 cup milk
2 egg yolks, slightly beaten

½ cup flaked coconut
½ teaspoon vanilla extract
¼ teaspoon almond extract
Butter

1.   In a medium saucepan, combine sugar, cornstarch, and salt. Gradually add milk, stirring constantly. Cook and stir over moderate heat until mixture thickens and begins to bubble. Remove from heat.

2.   Add a few tablespoons of hot mixture to egg yolks and stir to blend. Slowly pour warmed yolks into saucepan, stirring constantly. Cook and stir mixture over moderate heat until yolk mixture begins to bubble. Remove from heat. Stir in flaked coconut and vanilla and almond extracts.

3.   Transfer filling to bowl. Place a piece of buttered waxed paper directly on filling and cool to room temperature. Refrigerate at least 1 hour before using.

Yield: About 1 cup.

Grand Marnier Filling and Frosting

2 cups very cold heavy cream
1 cup sifted confectioners' sugar
2 tablespoons Grand Marnier

1 tablespoon finely grated orange peel

In a deep metal or glass bowl, and using electric beaters, beat cream, sugar, Grand Marnier, and orange peel on low speed until smooth and thick. Refrigerate until ready to use.

Yield: Enough to fill and frost an angel food or chiffon cake split crosswise into 3 layers.

Lemon Filling

4 egg yolks
6 tablespoons granulated sugar
3 tablespoons butter, cut into
  small pieces
½ cup strained, freshly squeezed
  lemon juice

2 teaspoons finely grated lemon
  peel
Butter

1. Combine yolks, sugar, butter, lemon juice, and peel in a heavy, non-aluminum saucepan. Cook and stir mixture over moderate heat, until mixture thickens and coats the back of a spoon. (Do not let mixture boil—it will curdle.)

2. Transfer filling to a small bowl. Place a piece of buttered waxed paper directly on filling and cool to room temperature. Refrigerate at least 1 hour before using.

Yield: About 1 cup.

Apricot Glaze

Use this to seal in the crumbs of a cake, or to make an unfrosted cake glisten.

1 cup apricot jam
2 teaspoons freshly squeezed
lemon juice

Heat jam in a small, heavy saucepan over low heat; stir frequently until dissolved (about 5 minutes). Remove from heat and stir in lemon juice. Use immediately. Unused glaze may be kept in a tightly covered jar in the refrigerator indefinitely. Reheat before using.

Yield: 1 cup.

Blueberry Sauce

2 cups fresh or thawed, frozen
   blueberries
½ cup granulated sugar
2 tablespoons freshly squeezed
   lemon juice

2 teaspoons grated lemon peel
1 tablespoon cornstarch

In a medium saucepan over moderate heat, combine berries, sugar, lemon juice, and peel with ¼ cup water. Bring to a boil; cook until berries burst. Combine cornstarch with 2 teaspoons water to make a smooth paste. Stir into berries and continue to boil until mixture looks clear and thickens (about 2 minutes). Serve warm or cold.

Yield: About 2 cups.

Fast Fudge Frosting

8 squares (8 ounces) semisweet
   chocolate, coarsely chopped

1 cup heavy cream
1 tablespoon rum (optional)

   1.   In the bowl of a food processor, and using the steel blade, process chocolate until finely chopped. (If using a blender, chop chocolate very fine; add hot cream, ¼ cup at a time, processing until smooth.)

   2.   In a small, heavy saucepan, heat cream just until tiny bubbles appear around edges of pan. Turn on food processor and pour hot cream through feed tube in a steady stream, processing until smooth. Blend in rum, if desired. Cool to room temperature without stirring; frosting will thicken as it cools.

Yield: Enough to fill and frost an 8- or 9-inch 2-layer cake, or to frost a 10-inch tube cake or a 9- by 13- by 2-inch cake.

Chocolate Glaze

2 squares (2 ounces) semisweet
  chocolate
2 tablespoons butter
¼ cup granulated sugar
2 tablespoons light corn syrup

Pinch salt
¼ cup heavy cream
2 teaspoons cornstarch
1 teaspoon vanilla extract

1. Combine chocolate, butter, sugar, corn syrup, and salt in a small, heavy saucepan. Cook over low heat, stirring occasionally until chocolate and butter melt and sugar dissolves.

2. Combine heavy cream and cornstarch in a measuring cup, stirring until well blended. Pour into chocolate mixture; cook over medium heat, stirring constantly until mixture begins to boil. Remove from heat; stir in vanilla. Cool glaze in pan 5 minutes, stirring occasionally, before pouring over cooled cake.

Yield: About ¾ cup.

Classic Fudge Frosting

4 squares (4 ounces) unsweetened
  chocolate
3 tablespoons butter
3 cups sifted confectioners' sugar

4 tablespoons milk
1 teaspoon vanilla extract
Pinch salt

1.   In the top part of a double boiler over simmering water, melt chocolate and butter, stirring occasionally until smooth. Remove top part of boiler; cool chocolate until warm to the touch.

2.   In a medium bowl, combine sugar, milk, vanilla, and salt, stirring until well blended. Stir in melted chocolate until thoroughly combined. Frosting will thicken as it cools; spread quickly on cooled cake. If frosting is too thick to spread, add 1 or 2 tablespoons additional milk.

Yield: About 2½ cups, or enough to fill and frost an 8- or 9-inch 2-layer cake.

Vanilla Cream Filling

6 tablespoons granulated sugar
2 tablespoons cornstarch
Pinch salt
1 cup milk
2 egg yolks, slightly beaten

1 tablespoon butter plus butter
  for greasing
½ teaspoon vanilla extract
Pinch ground cinnamon

1.   In a medium saucepan, combine sugar, cornstarch, and salt; gradually add milk, stirring constantly. Cook and stir over moderate heat until mixture thickens and begins to bubble. Remove from heat.

2.   Add a few tablespoons of hot mixture to egg yolks and stir to blend. Slowly pour warmed yolks into saucepan, stirring constantly.

3.   Cook and stir mixture over low heat until it begins to bubble. Remove from heat. Stir in butter, vanilla, and cinnamon.

4.   Transfer filling to bowl. Place a piece of buttered waxed paper directly on filling and cool to room temperature. Refrigerate at least 1 hour before using.

Yield: About 1 cup.

Raspberry-Peach Sauce

A delicious sauce to dish out with any plain cake.

2 packages (10 ounces each)
  frozen raspberries
¼ cup best-quality peach
` preserves

1 tablespoon kirsch
1 teaspoon cornstarch

  1.   Thaw raspberries according to directions on package; drain and reserve syrup.
  2.   In a medium bowl, combine raspberries, peach preserves, and kirsch; set aside.
  3.   In a small saucepan, stir together reserved raspberry syrup and cornstarch until well blended; cook, stirring constantly, over medium heat until mixture thickens (about 2 minutes).
  4.   Pour hot syrup over raspberry-peach mixture, stirring gently. Cool to room temperature. Cover, and chill thoroughly before using. Sauce may be frozen up to 6 months.

Yield: About 2 cups.

Lady Baltimore Frosting

1 *cup chopped raisins*
1 *cup chopped dried figs*
½ *cup sweet sherry or brandy*
1 *recipe 7-Minute Frosting (page 140)*

1½ *cups chopped pecans*
Chopped pecans, for garnish (optional)

1.   Soak raisins and figs in sherry for at least 2 hours or up to 3 days.

2.   On the day you plan to fill and frost the cake, prepare 7-Minute Frosting. When cool, divide frosting in half. Fold marinated fruit and pecans into one half; fill layers with this mixture. Frost top and sides of cake with remaining frosting. Sprinkle top of cake with additional chopped nuts, if desired.

Yield: Enough to fill and frost an 8- or 9-inch 3-layer cake.

Lane Filling

1 cup granulated sugar
8 egg yolks
⅓ cup bourbon or brandy
½ cup butter, softened

1 cup chopped figs
¾ cup flaked coconut
¾ cup chopped glacé cherries
¾ cup chopped pecans

1. In the top part of a double boiler over simmering water, combine sugar and yolks, stirring constantly until sugar dissolves and mixture thickens and coats the back of a spoon. Remove from heat; stir in bourbon. Cool to room temperature.

2. In a small bowl, and using electric beaters, cream butter until light and smooth. Blend in egg yolk mixture. Fold in figs, coconut, cherries, and pecans.

Yield: Enough to spread between layers of an 8- or 9-inch 3-layer cake.

Orange-Laced Chocolate Sauce

Serve this sauce hot or cold with angel food, chiffon, or pound cake.

¾ cup heavy cream
1 ounce milk chocolate
3 ounces white chocolate

Pinch salt
1 tablespoon Grand Marnier

Combine heavy cream, chocolates, and salt in a small, heavy saucepan over low heat, stirring frequently until chocolates melt and mixture is smooth. Remove from heat; stir in Grand Marnier.

Yield: About 1 cup.

Sweetened Whipped Cream

The best whipped cream is made with very cold, fresh, unpasteurized heavy or whipping cream. To facilitate beating, place beaters and mixing bowl in the freezer for at least 10 minutes before beating. Because heavy cream approximately doubles when whipped, to make 1 cup sweetened *whipped* cream, you would halve the ingredients in this recipe.

1 cup heavy cream
1 tablespoon confectioners' sugar
1 teaspoon vanilla extract

In a deep metal or glass bowl, and using electric beaters, beat cream, sugar, and vanilla on low speed until smooth and thick. Do not overbeat or cream will turn to butter. Refrigerate until ready to use.

Yield: About 2 cups.

Cream Cheese Frosting

This frosting is particularly delicious spread over carrot cake or banana layer cake.

8 ounces cream cheese, softened
1 cup butter, softened
2 cups sifted confectioners' sugar

1 teaspoon lemon juice or vanilla
*   extract*

In a medium bowl, beat together cream cheese and butter until smooth. Add confectioners' sugar, ¼ cup at a time, beating after each addition until mixture is smooth and fluffy. Beat in lemon juice.

Yield: About 3 cups, or enough to fill and frost an 8- or 9-inch 2-layer cake or to frost a 9- by 12- by 2-inch cake.

Chocolate-Dipped Strawberries

*3 squares (3 ounces) semisweet
    chocolate, coarsely chopped*
1 tablespoon unsalted butter

1 teaspoon orange liqueur
*18 strawberries, unhulled, with
    stem if possible*

1.   Combine chocolate, butter, and orange liqueur in a small custard cup or saucepan and set in a pan of hot water over low heat. Stir frequently until chocolate is melted. Remove from heat.

2.   Line a baking sheet with waxed paper. Dip a strawberry halfway into chocolate and place it on prepared sheet. Repeat with remaining berries. Refrigerate until set (about 10 minutes).

If you're not planning on using the dipped berries immediately, cover and store in a cool place for up to 1 day. (Don't store them in the refrigerator, however, because the chocolate will develop a pale, gray color known as "bloom." The chocolate will be okay to eat, but looks unappealing.)

Yield: 18 chocolate-dipped strawberries.

Index

162